SET UP TO FAIL:
100 THINGS WRONG WITH AMERICA'S SCHOOLS

by

Kathleen Loftus

"A child mis-educated is a child lost."

-- John F. Kennedy

Copyright © 2006 Kathleen P. Loftus
All rights reserved

Published by
Outcomes Educational Services
Buffalo Grove, IL   60089

ISBN # 978-0-6151-3474-1

This book can be purchased at www.lulu.com

The author can be contacted at
kploftus@outcomes4learning.com

To my kids, your kids, your neighbors' kids, and to all other kids in America who deserve, but have ever been denied, a quality education from their schools.

Preface

America's schools have an incomparable influence over the lives of virtually all of our nation's citizens. American parents are consumed with residing within the boundaries of the best school districts for their children that they can possibly afford. Even nonparent-homeowners are wholly dependent upon the performance of their local schools in determining the value of their homes, and, as such, their net worth. Parents who cannot afford to consider a broad range of residential options often suffer the most, with schools in America's less affluent areas consistently receiving the proverbial "short end of the stick," when it comes to educational excellence, despite the great strides toward equality that have been forged in virtually every other American institution. Even the schools in America's "better" neighborhoods are still fraught with enormous problems and blunders borne out of an antiquated structure and misplaced priorities that are no longer relevant, if they ever were.

Yet, in this "land of the free," compulsory education remains America's one bastion of "Communistic" governance. While Americans are free to bring children into this world and raise them more or less as they choose, the fact remains that on or around each child's 6th birthday all parents must surrender an enormous amount of their parental authority to their local neighborhood branch of their state's government; the local public school. Their alternatives are few, including paying dearly for private schools, or else sacrificing one wage-earner's salary to opt for home schooling. In no case is it permissible for parents to circumvent this intrusion of formalized education into their children's lives altogether.

This is not meant to suggest, however, that all forms of public school in America should be eliminated. The purpose of this book is simply to illustrate the enormity of influence America's schools have on parents' rights over their *own children*, while this compulsory American institution, which has evolved in both scope and governmental control in the last 100 years, actually still has much room for improvement.

Over seventy years after compulsory education became the law of the land, American educational leaders seem to have forgotten that they assumed this dictatorial position over parents' rights because of the original contention that they could do a *better* job. Nevertheless, although two-parent-wage-earner and single-parent households have been the norm in this country for over 35 years, America's schools are still required only to adhere to a daily and yearly schedule that was developed when the overwhelming majority of students came from two-parent, single-wage-earner households.

The point is this: If America is going to continue to require that all parents, except those with extraordinary means, send their children to these state-run institutions or risk being charged with neglect, imprisonment, or both, then they should *at least* ensure that these institutions are doing a *better* job than if the children did not attend school in the first place. Further, America's schools should not be requiring or condoning anything that has the potential to cause children any amount of emotional or cognitive injury. Unfortunately, much of what takes place today in America's schools was established to meet social, economic, and educational conditions that were present nearly a century ago.

Each day, as new babies are born in America, their parents vow to watch over them and to protect them from all harm. Yet, in only a few short years, these parents will be required to surrender them to an institution that will often care more about maintaining order and controlling costs than helping their children grow into knowledgeable and productive citizens. This is neither fair nor is it American. Like no other organization in the country, America's educational system holds the key to our nation's entire sociological, economic, and political future. Unfortunately, few government leaders appear to recognize this, with even fewer being sufficiently knowledgeable or empowered to effect needed change to this once innovative, but now largely antiquated, institution.

Still, one of the biggest obstacles to effective schools in America is that so many of those involved in their management and oversight are largely unaware of the particular knowledge, experiences, perspectives, difficulties, and needs of the other stakeholders. From the students, to the teachers, to the administrators, to the parents, to the community members, each has separate and distinct needs rarely considered by the rest. One only has to examine America's schools' stagnating test scores, growing dropout rates, increasing student assaults, (not to mention teacher assaults), combined with ever-increasing parental frustration, to realize that America's schools are not living up to their implied premise: That they exist to do a better job of educating America's kids than most parents.

The various issues addressed in this book are intended to bridge some of these gaps in awareness and understanding, while telling it like it *really* is in America's schools today in plain language, and not the scholarly theoretical jargon of most other books addressing school failures, so that all may gain some greater understanding of this national crisis. America's school system has managed to maintain an illusion of responsibility, but this illusion is largely dependent upon the ignorance of the American public. Only the most educated and informed parents have been able to successfully navigate schools' complex network in order to ensure that their children receive all of the educational services to which they are legally entitled. In the majority of America's schools there exists an overriding condition of chaos, pathos, irresponsibility, and failure, threatening to seriously erode the very fiber of the nation.

One of the most glaring aspects of this book, you will find, is its many contradictions. As with any organization that seeks to be all things to all people, there are multiple forces, multiple priorities, and multiple perspectives all coming together in America's schools in a way that evokes both collaboration and conflict. On one page you may see teachers' unions being blamed for limiting schools' options, while on another this dilemma is being attributed to school administrator demands on teachers. That's part of the problem. America's schools today are comprised of multiple groups with conflicting, and sometimes directly opposing, goals.

Nevertheless, it is hoped that Americans everywhere whose lives are being affected in some way by America's current educational system will find some insight they can use to encourage improvements in the policymaking, leading, and development of America's schools in the near future. It is further hoped that this book will serve to remove much of the cloak of secrecy and intimidation associated with a system occupying the majority of American children's from babyhood to adulthood.

- k.l.

TABLE OF CONTENTS

THE "MISSION:"
"WHAT DO THEY *THINK* THEY'RE DOING? – 1

1. "MISSION STATEMENTS"
2. CONFLICTING SCHOOL AGENDAS
3. LACK OF A UNIFIED SCHOOL PLAN
4. MEANINGLESS "LEARNING GOALS"
5. THE MYTH OF "SCHOOL CHOICE"
6. "COLLEGE OR BUST"
7. PLEDGE OF "MISUNDERSTANDING"
8. KIDS: LEAVE YOUR RIGHTS AT THE DOOR
9. UNEQUAL SCHOOL FUNDING
10. SCHOOLS ARE NOT MEDICAL CLINICS
11. TEACHERS ARE NOT PSYCHIATRISTS
12. REAL *PARENTS CARE*
13. SCHOOL PARENTS GET NO RESPECT
14. PERPETUATION OF A SOCIAL CASTE SYSTEM
15. NEIGHBORHOOD SCHOOLS ~
OK FOR GOOD NEIGHBORHOODS
16. SO, WHAT'S THE REAL POINT OF SCHOOL?
17. ATHLETIC vs.
ACADEMIC ACHIEVEMENT

THE FORMAT:
"WHAT'S GOING ON HERE?"

18. TOO MUCH TO DO ANYTHING WELL
19. ONE SIZE FITS SOME
20. TOO MANY CHANGES
21. DISCIPLINE = VACATION
(or TEACHERS ARE NOT THE POLICE)
22. SCHOOL SCHEDULES:
A BURDEN ON THE PARENTS
23. A "PRISON MENTALITY"

24. UNREALISTIC CLASS SIZES
25. DISCRETIONARY FUNDS & UNEQUAL GRANTS
26. DEPARTMENTAL COMPETITION = PERFORMANCE ISOLATION
27. NEGATIVE PRESSURES ON "MISFITS"
28. GIFTED = AVERAGE, AVERAGE = SLOW
29. DE-EMPHASIS ON STANDARDIZED TESTS
30. ATHLETICS: THE SELLING OF A SCHOOL'S SOUL
31. TRYOUTS DENY STUDENTS THEIR RIGHTS
32. SCHOOLS' BEHAVIORAL EXPECTATION: "GIRLS"
33. UNEQUAL INSTRUCTION AND OTHER SCHOOL SERVICES
34. NO ADVANCED PLACEMENT ART CLASSES
35. GRADE "LEVELS" OFTEN UNBALANCED
36. HIGH SCHOOL GRADUATES WHO CAN'T PASS COLLEGE ENTRANCE EXAMS
37. NO GRADE-TO-GRADE COLLABORATION

**THE LEADERSHIP: MISGUIDED
"WHO DO THEY THINK THEY ARE?"**

38. SCHOOLS' AUTHORITY: IN LOCO PARENTIS (OR: "DRIVING THE PARENTS CRAZY")
39. TOO MUCH FUNDING SECRECY
40. THE "SQUEAKY WHEEL" APPROACH TO "CUSTOMER" SERVICE
41. PRINCIPALS ONLY KNOW ABOUT THEIR "REGULAR ED" STUDENTS
42. THE SUPERINDENTS: "OUR WAY OR THE (VACATION) HIGHWAY"
43. STATE DEPARTMENTS OF (TOO LITTLE) EDUCATION
44. AMERICA'S SCHOOLS HAVE TOO MANY "COOKS"

45. TEACHER "EVALUATIONS"
THE ANNUAL "DOG & PONY SHOW"
45. RIGHT HAND, LEFT HAND, WHOSE HAND?

**THE TEACHERS
(AND OTHER SCHOOL STAFF):**
"WHAT GIVES THEM THE RIGHT?"

47. TEACHER "TRAINING"
48. NO OWNERSHIP FOR STUDENT LEARNING
49. UNION RULES: "THE UNION RULES!"
50. TEACHING WITH A' "TEAMSTER" MENTALITY
51. AUTOMATIC RAISES:
WHETHER OR NOT KIDS LEARN
52. INSTRUCTION BASED ON
TEACHER CONVENIENCE,
53. COED LOCKER ROOMS
AND SAME-SEX ATTRACTION
54. TEACHERS CAN'T BE REASSIGNED
(IF THEY DON'T WANT TO BE)
55. TEACHERS SHORTENED WORK YEAR -
PLUS "PLANNING PERIODS"
56. GUIDANCE COUNSELORS:
TOO FEW FOR TOO MANY
57. TEACHERS' AIDES:
THE LEAST-TRAINED TO DO THE MOST

THE FACILITIES:
"WHAT KIND OF PLACE IS THIS?"

58. MOST SCHOOLS CONTAIN
MULTIPLE HAZARDS
59. SCHOOL BATHROOMS:
UNFIT FOR PUBLIC USE
60. NO AIR CONDITIONING!!!

61. SCHOOL BUSES:
PARENTS' WORST NIGHTMARE
62. SCHOOL LIBRARIES: IT'S NOT THE 50'S
63. SCHOOL LOCKER ROOMS: IT'S NOT THE 60'S
64. SCHOOL COMPUTER LABS: IT'S NOT THE 70'S
65. NO "PREMISES LIABILITY"

THE INSTRUCTION:
"HOW COULD THEY?"

66. NO INSTRUCTIONAL CONSISTENCY
67. TEACHING IS AT THE TEACHERS' DIREECTION
68. NO GRADE-TO-GRADE ARTICULATION
69. "SCHEDULED THINKING"
70. NO "LIGHT AT THE END OF THE TUNNEL"
71. "LATE" WORK PENALIZED:
BUT IT'S STILL LEARNING!!
72. SUBJECT KNOWLEDGE
DOES NOT GUARANTEE AN ABILITY TO TEACH
73. QUASHED NATURAL TENDANCIES
74. LEARNING AT KIDS' OWN PACE IS PENALIZED
75. STUDENTS' OWN INTERESTS NOT PART OF
THE "LESSON PLAN"
76." TEACHING" EQUALS
(MERELY) "PRESENTING"
77. PE: A HUGE WASTE OF TIME & TEACHERS
78." CHEATING" vs. MAKING LEARNING EASIER
79. INCORRECT & IRRESPONSIBLE INSTRUCTION
80. HOMEWORK: SCHOOLS'
ULTIMATE INTRUSION
81. INSTRUCTION WITH NO
LONG-RANGE OBJECTIVES
82. LESSONS NOT BASED ON STUDENTS' NEEDS
83. ADULT LIVING SKILLS NOT TAUGHT
84. SPECIAL EDUCATION: "WHAT'S SO SPECIAL?"

85. *"DISABILITY" MEANS
"DISCARDED EXPECTATIONS"*
86. *MISIDENTIFICATION, OVER-IDENTIFICATION,
UNDER-EDUCATION*
87. *SPECIAL EDUCATION "INCLUSION"
NO ONE PREPARED THE
"INCLUDING" TEACHERS*

**THE STUDENTS:
"WHO'S REALLY RESPONSIBLE?"**

88. *"NO ONE GRADES THE TEACHERS"*
89. *TEACHERS CAN'T OR WON'T BE RESPONSIBLE*
90. *PARENTS GET NO GOVERNMENTAL
PROTECTION*
91. *PARENTS' RIGHTS:
KEPT HIDDEN FROM VIEW*
92. *REGIONAL OFFICES OF EDUCATION:
"ARTIFICIAL" AUTHORITIES*
93. *TEACHER MALPRACTICE AND
OTHER "CRIMES" AGAINST STUDENTS*

THE OUTCOMES: "WHAT GOOD IS IT?"

94. *ARBITRARY PROMOTIONS*
95. *GRADES BASED ON BEHAVIOR, NOT LEARNING*
96. *A "D" IS GOOD ENOUGH*
97. *UNEQUAL GRADUATION REQUIREMENTS*
98. *STUDENT FAILURES ARE NEVER THE
TEACHERS' FAULT*
99. *"REINVENTING THE WHEEL"
WASTES TIME AND TALENT*
100. *AMERICA'S SCHOOLS: WHAT'S REALLY
THE POINT?*

"I am not an advocate for frequent and untried changes in laws and <u>constitutions</u> . . . but laws and <u>institutions</u> must go hand in hand with the progress of the human mind. As that becomes more developed, more enlightened, as new discoveries are made, new truths disclosed, and manners and opinions change with the change of circumstances, institutions must advance also, and keep pace with the times. We might as well require a man to wear still the same coat which fitted him when a boy, as civilized society to remain ever under the regimen of their barbarous ancestors."

-- *Thomas Jefferson, July 12, 1810*

THE "MISSION"

"WHAT DO THEY <u>THINK</u> THEY'RE DOING?"

1.

"MISSION STATEMENTS"

Each separate school district in America operates like a franchise, only with far less accountability and direction from headquarters than is required to manage a typical 7-Eleven store. Oh, there are rules and requirements, but few that actually have anything to do with teaching and learning. For example, each district, and sometimes each individual school within these districts, is required by their state education agencies to have an official "mission statement." This declaration is meant to reflect a school's focus and intentions. Now, all schools in America are bound by the same federal education regulations. How curious, then, that these proclamations should be *required* to differ from one school to the next. Parents might even be justified in bringing suit if their children's school promises "One student body, one curriculum," while the school across town boasts, "Each student will discover his or her own unique gifts."

Shouldn't all schools in America have the same mission: To educate all its students in the knowledge and skills that will enable them to be thoughtful, productive, contented, and socially-responsible adults? And, isn't the knowledge for which schools hold the greatest monopoly primarily concentrated in Reading, Writing, Mathematics, Foreign Languages, History, and the Sciences? Further, aren't the learning needs of children virtually the same throughout the country? Is there really a difference between the instructional requirements of students in Oregon and those in North Carolina, or anywhere in between? Why, then, should America's schools be wasting any amount of energy or resources developing individual school mission statements?

This is just one of countless unnecessary undertakings expended by individual schools in the name of creating the "illusion of care" that is repeated in many forms. Ironically, this particular practice of "reinventing the wheel" at taxpayer expense by America's schools, in the name of "serving" students, is one that is then almost completely ignored by school staff. It's merely a slogan to adorn letterheads and school foyers; while almost never having any real affect whatsoever on actual school practices or decisions.

READ MORE FROM BLOOMINGTON, INDIANA:

Mission, Vision & Delusion in Schooling

http://www.newfoundations.com/EGR/VisionDelusion.html

SOLUTION 1:

HAVE JUST ONE NATIONAL SCHOOL MISSION STATEMENT, WITH NOT <u>ONE</u> ADDITIONAL TAX DOLLAR PAID TO THE SALARIES OF SCHOOL EMPLOYEES TO DEVELOP "NEW" AND "IMPROVED" VERSIONS OF THESE UNNECESSARY SLOGANS.

2.

CONFLICTING SCHOOL AGENDAS

To begin with, America's schools exist for a number of reasons, but these reasons are neither specified anywhere, nor standardized by any region or group. They are not prescribed by the Constitution, nor mandated by any federal law. Each faction of individuals responsible for governing, administrating, implementing, and utilizing America's schools seem to have a different, and often conflicting, purpose and agenda that is also frequently misunderstood by the other groups.

Those responsible for school's governance, (e.g. the U.S. Department of Education and the 51 State Education Agencies), appear to view their roles as that of philosophers, handing down tenets and directives to their humble and grateful masses who are only too eager to comply with their superior insight for the children's greater good. School district administrators view themselves as shepherds leading a group of uninformed and self-serving "child-adults," (the teachers), who are incapable of individual decision-making. The teachers, in turn, see themselves as independent contractors, repressed by misguided administrators who do not understand or appreciate their efforts or their numerous difficulties.

The students and parents expect all of the other factions involved in the educational process to with be selfless benefactors devoted solely to improving the lives of America's future citizens. They presume, at least initially, an absence of favoritism, detrimental experience, or ill will. Parents, in particular, assume that, since they are compelled by law to surrender their children to this enormous government body, that this organization will act cooperatively toward the best interests of their own and all other children. They further expect, from their state and the federal governments, that a system of accountability and protectiveness is in place to safeguard and uphold all children's educational rights. Unfortunately, no "AMA" (American Medical Association) level of oversight exists in American education such as exists in the field of medicine.

In recent years, with the enactment of Special Education laws, the lack of governmental accountability for education has become only clearer. Parents throughout the land have come to know that the laws theoretically in place to protect their children's educational rights are largely insufficient to ever accomplish this feat, and that governmental overseers know it. There are few financial penalties in place to compel schools' legal compliance with America's education laws. Nevertheless, many medical mistakes may actually be more easily reversed than some educational ones, due to missed developmental learning milestones. Yet, no system of educational malpractice recovery exists in America.

READ MORE FROM DALLAS, TEXAS:

http://www.zwire.com/site/news.cfm?BRD=1994&dept_id=339096&newsid=13412610&PAG=461&rfi=9

SOLUTION 2:

PUBLICIZE THE NUMBER AND NATURE OF SCHOOL COMPLAINTS, ALONG WITH HOW EACH WAS RESOLVED, WHILE HOLDING BOTH SCHOOLS AND INDIVIDUAL EDUCATORS LEGALLY LIABLE FOR INSTRUCTIONAL MALPRACTICE.

3.

LACK OF A UNIFIED SCHOOL PLAN

One of the major trends in public education in the past 25 years has been toward "site-based management." This refers to the deferral of much of the decision-making in schools from state and local administrators to the individual districts or schools. Unfortunately, without a common plan, the disparity of education from city to city, from district to district, even from school to school within the same district can, and often does, vary significantly. Sure, there are unified state learning goals, teacher-credentialing requirements, and other legal constraints related to budgeting, facilities management, and enrollment practices. Nevertheless, school systems as a whole have maintained a lack of capacity or desire for a unified national curriculum. Such a concept would have the potential to streamline instruction and remove many of the difficulties related to student transfers. Still, this option has been dismissed as too controlling and limiting of individual school systems, while also considered too difficult to uphold.

Nevertheless, the current lack of school uniformity makes it very difficult for America's very mobile society, for students, parents, or the schools themselves, to successfully manage student transfers. The recently-enacted school self-reporting legislation even acknowledges schools' student mobility rate a condition of exceptional circumstance requiring greater consideration. Having a high number of students moving in and out of a given school is recognized as having a negative effect on student academic achievement. Would this still be the case if the students were simply moving from one 5th grade class to another within, say, the same building? Probably not. Why, then, should this be so different when students move from school to school within, theoretically, the same American public school system?

Since the U.S. Department of Education acknowledges student mobility to be a detriment, doesn't it stand to reason, then, that efforts would be welcomed that would counteract this problem? Unfortunately, as will be shown over and over throughout this book, instead of adopting a more "corporate" mentality focused on producing successful outcomes, America's school systems continually cling to old ways, particularly whenever they can escape change by simply blaming the parents.

In this case, parents who must move frequently are "punished" by America's schools, along with their children. Rather than providing a compulsory educational system that ensures student success, America's schools continue to "punish" parents who need to work, while rewarding those who do not. Further, those who need to relocate to another area of the country are treated as simply "on their own," when it comes to finding compatible and appropriate education for their children in their new location. Teachers would argue that they could not possibly be expected to be on the same page, in the same book as all other schools within the same grade-level in America. This would not, they argue, account for individual student needs, or other local factors. Ironically, one of the only other institutions in this country that has managed to overcome this purported difficulty with establishing uniformity of lessons within a prescribed timeline is the Catholic Church. While meaning to bestow no particular acclaim to this, or any other religion, one cannot discuss America's schools without recognizing the second largest K-12 educational organization in

America, with schools and churches of various sizes and demographics throughout America that has also, somehow, managed to find a way to impart a prescribed single body of knowledge to an extensive and diverse assemblage of people on a weekly basis. In addition to their record of superior achievement scores of their school students, on any given Sunday, in any Roman Catholic Church anywhere in the world, in hundreds of different languages, they are, nevertheless, *all on the same page!* As a result, one can travel from one church to the next throughout not just America, but *the world,* and not miss the chronology of the series of scripture lessons that serve as the basis for the rest of the service called the Mass. Priests are permitted some leeway with regard to their homily, (a personal message illustrating principles that support the prescribed scriptures), but are not given full license to teach whatever they choose. There is also a degree of flexibility, within limits, with regard to the hymns sung, versions of prayers recited, and announcements read.

Using this example, imagine the benefits to students and parents across the land if they were no longer hampered by the inconsistencies in curricula they encounter when moving from city to city or state to state. Imagine, also, the greater ease to administrators if what was being taught were tied to a very specific prescribed timeline and content. At one time there was no need in this country for a national curriculum. Students residing in Virginia might never encounter many of the circumstances awaiting students in New Mexico. No longer is this the case. As our society becomes ever more global, our need for educational equity grows only more necessary.

READ MORE FROM IOWA CITY, IOWA:

"There is a district level vision and a classroom level vision, but no linkage between the two. The system is so large—different departments have different visions and goals. Compounding that is the fact that technology changes every day."

http://www.ncrel.org/engauge/framewk/vis/comm/viscomin.htm

AND

From the United Kingdom:

National Curriculum

"The National Curriculum was introduced to ensure that all children in State schools receive the same basic education. Ten subjects must be taught in primary schools. They are divided up into Core and Foundation subjects."

http://www.parents.org.uk/national.htm

SOLUTION 3:

ESTABLISH A NATIONAL CURRICULUM AND REQUIRE EVERY SCHOOL IN AMERICA TO TEACH THE SAME LESSON ON THE SAME DAY IN THE SAME GRADE.

4.

MEANINGLESS "LEARNING GOALS"

As part of a move toward national learning standards to offset potential inequities between regions, most states have adopted standardized learning goals for each subject and grade level, to be adhered to by their public schools in establishing district curriculum. The problem is that most of these goals are far too vague and open-ended to have any real effect on what students are actually being taught. Further, in most cases, these goals make no distinction between *skill development* and *knowledge acquisition.* For example, learning to read, not unlike learning to play an instrument, first requires sufficient mastery of the applicable "code," or language. One would not expect a student to learn only a few notes and symbols of the scale each year but then be using this same code to evaluate rhythm and cadence of Chopin at the same time, yet this is the logic schools use in expecting students who haven't yet been taught to read to benefit from social studies and science classes.

Another problem with most schools in America is their emphasis on equal time – not for the *students*, but for teachers and subjects. Too often, regardless of students' acquired levels of reading or math computation skills, they will almost never be permitted extra time beyond that which the pre-determined daily schedule prescribes, while concurrently affording equal time to "physical education," "music," "computer lab" and other seemingly less pressing needs. Even students placed in special education services supposedly designed to allow for different learning rates, are usually still held to these strict time parameters for receiving instruction.

Additionally, while one might expect that these learning goals would clearly define the mastery levels required for a child to be able to be promoted into the next grade level; this is simply not the case. Each subject area, (e.g. Math, Reading, Writing, etc.), contains at least three separate levels of performance: "Primary," "Intermediate," and "Advanced." Each of these performance benchmarks is written to be so general that almost any level of performance could apply, as desired. These "state learning goals," like many other school requirements, are perceived by most educators to simply be the "official" suggested curricula, not actually meant to be taken literally. This unspoken understanding is further upheld by the fact that almost nothing a teacher might or might not teach could actually have the potential to subject them to educational malpractice using these standards, not that any actual oversight of the delivery of these standards ever takes place. The only official supervision that even occurs related to teacher adherence to these standards is when school administrators are evaluating new or non-tenured teachers. However, these observations require much advance notice to the teachers, are limited in time and scope, while focused more on "classroom management" of the students than on the content being imparted to them. Knowing well in advance of the day and time of one's observation, few teachers have difficulty ensuring that their teaching "performance" includes all prescribed areas of instruction, even if it never does otherwise.

Curiously, much of American schools' public policies appear far more complicated than necessary. While employing complex and vague learning goals that are largely misunderstood by both teachers and parents alike, America's schools are, at the same time required to produce more and more standardized measures of student achievement that assess both student knowledge acquisition and learning progress. Clearly, the authors of these assessments have managed to establish clear and precise benchmarks of instruction for each grade-level. Yet, recent studies have shown that most state's mandated learning goals do not even align with the standardized assessments most are using to measure the progress of their students. It is beyond comprehension to understand why America's state departments of education cloud their learning benchmarks with more vague and complex definitions than necessary.

READ MORE FROM WISCONSIN CENTER FOR EDUCATION RESEARCH:

Critical Issue: Integrating Assessment and Instruction in Ways That Support Learning

http://www.ncrel.org/sdrs/areas/issues/methods/assment/as500.htm

---

SOLUTION 4:

STANDARDIZE GRADE-LEVEL LEARNING GOALS FOR ALL SUBJECTS, WHILE MAKING THEM MORE CONTENT-SPECIFIC. IF STUDENTS SHOULD BE DIVIDING FRACTIONS IN 6TH GRADE, THEN ONE OF THE 6TH GRADE MATH GOALS SHOULD SAY SO, INSTEAD OF USING WORDING THAT COULD BE SUBJECT TO MULTIPLE INTERPRETATIONS AND EXPECTATIONS.

5.

THE MYTH OF "SCHOOL CHOICE"

In a drastic effort to curtail the rapidly-increasing number of student-failures, (*Note: These are never referred to as "teacher-failures"*), the federal government, under President George W. Bush, enacted the "Elementary and Secondary Education Act," better known as the "No Child Left Behind Act," or NCLB. One of the most radical aspects of this legislation is the stipulation that if schools that are identified as failing to meet minimum student performance standards, fail to improve their performance consistent with prescribed benchmarks and timelines, parents are to be permitted to choose another school for their children. Sounds good, right?

Unfortunately, almost before the ink was dry on this new law, state and local educational systems around the country were seizing upon means to employ loopholes to this directive to protect their own interests. In the Chicago Public Schools, (CPS), for example, (one of the largest school systems in the country, having over 600 schools, more than a 1/2 a million students, and employing over 35,000 teachers), the administration moved quickly to impose limits on their parents' "choices" to those of the District's own design. The CPS system is divided into six separate regions geographically. Region 1 is located on the most elite north side, Region 6 on the most depressed south side, although many schools on the city's near west side regions have grown equally disparate. Schools in the more depressed regions are known to have a shortage in instructional resources and teaching talent, while schools in the more affluent regions of the *same district* enjoy classrooms full of unused materials and ample resources. How this can be, one might ask. Didn't mandated School Report Cards eliminate schools' ability to conceal any inequities? Not quite.

While those familiar with these annual school reports may have noticed is that school demographic data is reported by *school*, such as gender, racial, and socioeconomic makeup, while the really important stuff, including teacher qualifications and per pupil expenditure, are reported only as average figures by *school district*! This means that a school district may actually be expending several thousand more dollars per pupil at one school over another while reporting only the average expenditure for all schools in the district. Sadly, they get away with this legally since the law compelling the reporting of this data is actually worded, "Information must be reported per school *and/or* district." While likely intended specifically to include "one-school" districts, an untold number of other school systems have elected to report test scores and student information by school, but have then deliberately changed their methods mid-report by providing only district averages for the information they chose to conceal from parents and others.

READ MORE FROM:
"ALLIANCE FOR SCHOOL CHOICE:"
NCLB Choice = No Choice

http://www.edspresso.com/2006/05/nclb_choice_no_choice_neal_mcc.htm

SOLUTION 5:

REQUIRE THAT ALL SCHOOL AND STUDENT EXPENDITURES BE REPORTED BY SCHOOL, AND NOT MERELY BY DISTRICT, WHILE ALLOWING PARENTS THE OPPORTUNITY TO MAKE TRULY INFORMED SCHOOL CHOICES.

6.

"COLLEGE OR BUST"

Prior to World War II, typically only the elite 15% of American youth attended college, with even fewer graduating. Nevertheless, almost everybody worked, (all the men, anyhow). Unemployment insurance, welfare, and social security were unheard of. Making one's way in the world was not only an expectation; it was the only means of survival. Surely, there were many brilliant individuals who never had the benefit of a college education who could have benefited from one. However, there are likely just as many for whom college would have failed to meet their needs. They were best-suited for occupations requiring mechanical, technical, sales, or physical performance skills for which college would have only been a hindrance or, at least, unnecessary. This is very equally the case with many of their grandchildren and great-grandchildren today. Americans, as a whole, have not evolved sufficiently in the past 60 years to now be this intellectual and ethereal thinking mass, with none of us having any capacity or inclination toward careers in auto repair, cosmetology, retail, customer service, cooking, cleaning, garbage collection, machining, manufacturing, child care, or any of the many areas of construction. These are all still viable, respectable careers where an individual can earn a decent and steady wage without benefit of a four-year degree. Nevertheless, many school systems, CPS included, have adopted high school graduation standards designed only to accommodate the college preparatory track one option for all of its students. Those who cannot make the grade are left to drop out or fail.

In order to receive a high school diploma from most high schools in America, one's transcript must indicate the completion of Algebra, Geometry, Advanced Algebra/Trigonometry, English Literature, Organic Chemistry, and two years of the same Foreign Language. In addition to being an impractical standard for some students, this requirement actually exceeds states' minimum high school graduation requirements. This means that students attending a state-funded public high school in one regional area are sometimes held to a higher standard for high school completion than those residing in another system boundary within the same state.

Now, if these strict college-prep minimum standards could be shown to truly propel the majority of students toward greater academic achievement, they might actually be worthwhile. Instead, the undesired effects of holding all students to the same, often unrealistic standard are twofold: First, a significant number of students who might be able to achieve a viable and productive post-secondary career, given appropriate coursework and guidance are, instead, dropping out of high school in droves following multiple failures in too-stringent courses for which they are ill-suited. Secondly, and even worse, a number of schools are providing instruction to students that falls far short of that normally attributed to these course titles, with many parents being none the wiser. Those designated for "special education," regardless of learning potential, are being documented as having completed each of these college-bound courses in order to ensure that they graduate without further costs to the schools, when they are instead, unofficially, being placed into undocumented course substitutions such as "Basic Math," and "General Science," without any amount of tracking of the students' progress within this unofficial remedial instruction. This practice has even greater significance because special education students are eligible to remain at high school until age 21 if they have failed to meet all of their schools' requirements for graduation. By knowingly artificially documenting their completion of the required courses, schools are also circumventing this added expense, at the expense of students' legal rights.

Today's schools, like most other institutions, are most fervently driven by money. Not compassion, not dedication, not pedagogy, not academic excellence, *money*. And where does an overwhelming chunk of a school's disposable cash come from? A good deal comes from its sports programs. One of the key underlying basis for America's schools espousing these often unrealistically stringent graduation requirements for *all* its students, above even "official" state graduation requirements is not so much a desire for all of its students to qualify for college, but for all of its students to qualify for *college sports.*. Today, most American schools' graduation requirements do not so much match state and federal guidelines as those of the National Collegiate Athletic Association, (NCAA). The federal government requires that this organization impose these more stringent academic standards for athletes receiving athletic scholarships. As a result, school systems throughout America have adopted these arbitrary requirements of *all* their students. Unfortunately, in order to not be burdened with retaining the millions of students who will likely never pass all of these courses, those who do not drop out are simply passed along and then graduated while only demonstrating minimal skills not compatible with "Advanced Algebra," "Trigonometry," or other prescribed courses. In other words, so as to not stand in the way of possibly one Michael Jordan for every 1 million students, *all* of America's students are subject to being pushed through school with artificial grades on their transcripts, for artificial completion of artificial classes. Unfortunately, for the majority of these students who seek college admission based solely on academics and not athletic ability, they soon find that many of their "completed" courses do not come close to preparing them to pass even basic college admission tests at General Educational Development (GED) standards. Nevertheless, this practice is allowed to continue with the full knowledge and approval of most state departments of education, as well as most colleges and universities throughout the America. Colleges have little to lose as they can simply charge parents more for the needed extra remedial courses, but these parents have been ripped off. According to the high school transcripts of many students subsequently required to take extra remedial courses in college, many have documentation that they already sufficiently mastered the same material for which they are subsequently unable to demonstrate minimal mastery. They and their parents have been victims of a lie, yet no system of accountability exists within America's schools for parents to seek either punitive or monetary justice for these intentional acts of omission.

READ MORE FROM SEATTLE, WASHINGTON: The new "K-16" education movement
http://www.kimberlyswygert.com/archives/001666.html

SOLUTION 6:

SCHOOLS MUST ACKNOWLEDGE STUDENTS' ACTUAL PERFORMANCE ABILITIES, MAKE GREATER CORRELATIONS BETWEEN STUDENTS' STANDARDIZED ACHIEVEMENT SCORES AND THEIR "LETTER GRADES" WHILE GIVING STUDENTS PERFORMING BELOW GRADE LEVEL THE REMEDIATION THEY NEED, AND NOT MERELY PLACE THEM INTO CLASSES WITH "FAKE" COURSE TITLES.

7.

PLEDGE OF "MISUNDERSTANDING"

Interspersed with some of the more serious problems with America's schools are some that are simply exasperating. One such matter is the compulsory recitation of the "Pledge of Allegiance," recited by common practice in America's schools for many years, but has now been recently signed into law by G.W. Yet, this rather short verse, is not part of the Constitution, not tied to any meaningful historical event, but is simply a poem written by a journalist for *Liberty Magazine* in 1947. Sure, it's a nice little platitude *if that's what you choose to believe.* But, the very act of *requiring* its pronouncement completely opposes the very sentiment that its author sought to express. Since its daily recitation by all students being made a public school requirement in 2003, some degree of public controversy has arisen over the mention of the words *"under God."* Yet, these words were not even added to the piece until 1953, which, being a public school requirement, represents a clear "separation of church and state issue. Still, *that's not even the biggest problem with making this a requirement.*

Sadly one of the biggest contemporary tragedies in America is the rapid erosion of the English language, easily detected in the speech of today's youth, heard frequently in countless commercials, and has even made its way to the White House. A one-sentence passage that America, as a nation, clings to so passionately that we've even agreed to its being forcibly spoken aloud every day by all students in America, is now *not even punctuated properly.* On countless school and governmental documents on which the "Pledge" is printed, the comma appears in the *wrong place!* Part of this gaffe was actually caused, it would appear, by the very insertion of the words "*under God*" after the fact.

The following is an examination of the "Pledge" as it appears to have been originally intended by its author (Words in brackets were added for further clarity.)

It begins:

> "*I pledge allegiance to the flag of the United States of America and to the Republic for which it stands* [as] *one nation* [being] *indivisible with liberty and justice for all.*

Interpreting this further using more current terminology, it might read:

> "*I* [promise to be loyal] *to the flag of the United States of America and to the* [nation] [that it] *stands* [for], [a nation that is inseparable] *with* [freedom] *and* [fairness] *for all* [people].

Even re-inserting the words "*under God,*" does not drastically change the author's original intent; that our nation stands for complete freedom (*of choice?*) and fairness for all people. Adding the words, "*under God,*" is actually just the first of many governmental departures from the very freedom this "pledge" upholds, while being completely inconsequential to its intended message. It's not a pledge about the people of the United States having one God, as many have come to believe, it's about the fact that, we, as Americans, more so than the citizens of any other nation in the world, espouse the belief that we are meant to have *complete freedom* to do what we want, (*including how and where to educate our children?*), along with each citizen receiving *completely fair treatment.*

As far as the punctuation error, as the "Pledge" currently reads:

> "I pledge allegiance to the flag of the United States of America and to the Republic for which it stands, one nation under God, indivisible, (*Right Here! The comma after 'indivisible' does not belong!*) with liberty and justice for all."

By misplacing the comma what is actually being stated is that, as a nation, Americans are indivisible with *God*, not indivisible with liberty and justice, with these two virtues appearing to be tacked on as an afterthought, instead of being *the entire point* of the original sentiment! Still, properly punctuated, even with the inclusion of the words "*under God,*" it would still mean the following:

> I pledge allegiance [*promise to be loyal*] to the flag of the United States of America and to the Republic [*nation*] for which it stands [*that it stands for*], one nation {*under God*} indivisible [*inseparable*] with liberty [*freedom*] and justice [*fairness*] for all [*people*]. Get it?

READ MORE FROM THE U.S. SENATE:

Senators Call Pledge Decision 'Stupid'
http://archives.cnn.com/2002/ALLPOLITICS/06/26/senate.resolutio n.pledge/index.html

---

SOLUTION 7:

STOP FORCING AMERICA'S STUDENTS TO RECITE SOME MISUNDERSTOOD POEM (THAT ACTUALLY OPPOSES SUCH IMPOSTIONS ON PERSONAL FREEDOMS), WHILE REQUIRINING STUDENTS TO UTTER THE WORD "GOD," AS A GOVERNMENTALLY-COMPELLED PRAYER, EACH AND EVERY DAY.

8.

KIDS: LEAVE YOUR RIGHTS AT THE DOOR

One more point about the "pledge:" Not only is it misunderstood and misused, but neither it nor the U.S. Constitution (the *actual* American *law of the land*) are upheld by public schools. With very good reason, compulsory public schooling is not listed anywhere in the Constitution; not in the original Articles nor in *any* of its 27 Amendments. Yet, the majority of American parents, all but those who enjoy financial independence, would face certain jail time if they failed to surrender their children to the local school systems, for the better part of their kids' childhoods. Nevertheless, for these twelve or so years of compulsory schooling their children are, for the most part, considered exempt from the very rules that govern all other aspects of America and its citizens. Few American parents would stand for government officials coming into their homes and telling them how they may instruct, entertain, or communicate with their own children. However, it is precisely these same "parental" freedoms over America's children that are accorded equally to its schools. There is even a law specifically upholding schools' *parental* rights over students, superseding their own parents, called *"in loco parentis."* What this law does is grant all authority over America's children that most presume to be theirs alone, during the school day, while children are traveling to and from and attending school and, in some instances, during other times, as well. Within these non-democratic parameters occur countless instances of students' freedoms, (*the very freedoms to which schools demand daily verbal homage*), being blatantly and shamelessly denied them. Freedom of speech is probably the one violated most often, with students regularly being removed from their classrooms by school officials simply for exercising self-expression that is neither threatening nor harmful. Countless student due process rights are also routinely violated, as students are regularly "convicted" of offenses by their schools without benefit of any trial. In addition to this violating students' Constitutional rights, America's schools are also subject to their states' "school code," or other education regulations, most often consisting of a lengthy set of rights to which of each school-aged child is lawfully entitled. The most basic of these rights is each student's right to a free appropriate public education, or FAPE. Still, America's schools are not truly "free." Besides book fees, lab fees, and other miscellaneous charges tacked onto schools' cost of registration, of greater note are the monies expended for schools by many public school parents via their income, sales, and property taxes. Theoretically, if education were meant to be truly "free" for all students no parents of school-age children would have to pay any school taxes. America's schools are also far from "appropriate," unless it is educationally appropriate to expect each child to progress at the same rate as all other children born within a 12-month period in at least six separate subjects simultaneously.

READ MORE FROM SAN FRANCISCO, CALIFORNIA:
Federal Judge Rules Reciting Pledge in Schools Unconstitutional
http://www.foxnews.com/story/0,2933,169379,00.html

SOLUTION 8:

LET STUDENTS PROGRESS AT THEIR OWN PACE IN EACH SUBJECT AREA, IRRESPECTIVE OF THEIR BIRTHDAYS, AND STOP PENALZING THEM FOR A LACK OF "TIMELINESS" OF THEIR LEARNING

9.

UNEQUAL SCHOOL FUNDING

The whole process by which public schools are funded is quite complex and (intentionally?) mysterious. School district reporting of their expenditures *per school* is almost never done. Even if it was, there are still a number of variables to school funding that are largely undetectable to most Americans. Any attempt to explain the complex school funding formulas utilized by most states would likely cause most to stop reading further. Nevertheless, it is important for Americans to have at least a basic knowledge of public school finances, since, particularly for homeowners, school taxes generally comprise the greatest chunk of their property taxes. While schools receive their funding from a combination of sources, various states have different formulas and caps regarding how much money a particular district may raise above and beyond its state funding. Instead of being distributed equitably, what is clearly obvious is that students who attend schools in America's wealthy areas have no difficulty whatsoever raising sufficient funds to ensure optimal resources, facilities, and opportunities for students in every conceivable category, those in poorer districts struggle just to afford sufficient textbooks and desks.

READ MORE FROM MILWAUKEE, WISCONSIN:
The Return to Separate and Unequal
http://www.rethinkingschools.org/archive/15_03/Sep153.shtml

SOLUTION 9:

ESTABLISH MINIMUM SCHOOL STANDARDS IN ALL AREAS, FROM THE AGE OF TEXTBOOKS TO THE NUMBER OF CLASSROOMS WITH ALL SUPPLEMENTAL FUNDING LIMITED TO EXTRA-CURRICULUAR PROGRAMMING.

10.

SCHOOLS ARE NOT MEDICAL CLINICS

Somewhere back in the 1960's it was decided that parents could not always be relied upon to ensure that their children received proper vision care, as well as other medical services, when needed. For this reason, schools began conducting basic vision and hearing screenings, limited to assessing students utilizing the all-too familiar eye chart and other basic tools. At one time, these individual screenings were conducted by an actual "school nurse," with bona fide nursing credentials and a basic understanding of clinical procedures. This supplemental medical screening did likely catch a large percentage of students' sensory deficits. However, with the emergence of greater employment and childcare opportunities that followed, few holding nursing credentials choose school district employment in lieu of far more lucrative positions in medical facilities.

As a result, most schools, for the past 30 years or so, began substituting these professionals with "health clerks," capable of little more than checking a child's forehead for evidence of a fever, and calling parents at work to come and retrieve their children. Schools' continued use of the term "school nurse," is does little more than provide parents a false sense of security with regard to their children's safety while at school.

Nevertheless, schools continue to allow these untrained clerks to conduct these annual student screenings. Unfortunately, a large number of students who "pass" these assessments are only much later discovered to have significant sensory deficits that may have worsened, sometimes resulting in learning and processing deficits.

There is no way to know how many unsuspecting parents may have relied on these "screenings" that were never aware of their children's needs for appropriate medical intervention. Further, it is also not possible to know how many students have been diagnosed with learning disabilities that are simply the result of insufficient measurement of sensory perception.

Regardless of the number of missed diagnoses, however, schools are not subject to *any* penalties by the American Medical Association. School employees are not subject to the *Hippocratic Oath*. What only further compels schools' propensity for medical practice is the fact the many schools, while not medical facilities, regularly receive Medicaid funds for providing their unlicensed "medical" services.

On a related note, virtually all schools in America employ "school psychologists," individuals who, perhaps surprisingly, do not typically provide psychological counseling but are utilized primarily to conduct special education screenings. Unfortunately, in its noble effort to ensure that America's schools meet the needs of all of its students with disabilities it permitted these professionals with limited clinical training who are beholden first to their employers to make "clinical" diagnoses that affect their schools' bottom line. As a result, in far too many instances, millions of America's students appear to exhibit learning needs that were not "found" by their school's psychologist or, conversely, are relegated to segregated classrooms as a result of the findings of these "clinicians" that do not seem entirely warranted. Each school system has its own set of priorities when it comes to "difficult" students. Those with few resources encourage their school psychologists to find few, if any, learning deficits requiring costly supplemental services, while those with more spending flexibility have been known to compel them to "find anything" to justify the student being removed from the regular classroom.

READ MORE FROM NEW YOUR CITY:

"A recent investigation by the New York City Council Investigation Division found nearly two-thirds (63%) of the nonpublic schools surveyed have no full-time nurse; among those, half have no nurse at all."

http://www.nyc.gov/html/records/pdf/govpub/1118schoolnurses.pdf#search='no%20medical%20oversight%20of%20public%20schools'

SOLUTION 10:

IMMEDIATELY DISCONTINUE THE PRACTICE OF SCHOOLS PROVIDING ANY LEVEL OF MEDICAL OR PSYCHOLOGICAL SERVICES, OR ELSE SUBJECT THEM TO REGULAR SCRUTINY AND OVERSIGHT BY THE A.M.A.

11.

TEACHERS ARE NOT PSYCHIATRISTS

To continue this subject, besides assuming unqualified medical roles, educators have become less and less timid about expressing their *unqualified* medical diagnoses of students' *emotional* needs, as well. Once a taboo subject left only to the neuro-psychiatrists, today, countless teachers, school counselors, social workers, and others feel free to diagnose "Attention Deficit Hyperactivity Disorder" (ADHD), "Oppositional Defiant Disorder" (ODD), depression, and various other neurological conditions, including Autism. These "diagnoses" are often made simply as a result of the consensus of a formal meeting of various school staff, convened to determine a student's eligibility for special education services.

Now, on the surface, this may seem like a charitable extension of educator roles for the benefit of the students. The reality is quite the opposite. While special education services may have originally been devised as a means of assisting students with catching up to their non-disabled peers, today any special education eligibility almost always results in students being permanently limited from reaching grade-level academic goals, with "special education" having become equated with "permissible lowered expectations." Therefore, and more importantly, any diagnosis of special learning or behavioral needs, particularly those of a neuro-biological nature, should only be made by qualified physicians, subject to the standards of the profession.

Even the many potential deficits to students' cognitive abilities would be better assessed by non-school professionals. Unfortunately, an often too common practice in America's schools is for the diagnostic integrity of the "school psychologist" to be controlled by the whims and pocketbooks of school district administration. Fox example, a diagnosis of a learning disability is made theoretically based on evidence of a discrepancy between a child's learning potential, (I.Q.), and actual academic achievement. Only to qualify, students with *average or higher I.Q.'s*, having clear deficits in their performance when compared to their abilities, actually meet this federally-mandated criteria. Too often, however, students with environmental deficits, native language limitations, instructional gaps, or mental impairments, are "declared" LD by their school's psychologist, at the behest of their superiors, in order to solve any number of instructional, school achievement, or budgeting problems. Further, students with cognitive impairments, as well as those with severe emotional needs, are sometimes intentionally misdiagnosed as "learning disabled" simply because this eligibility is both easier to staff, while also being subject to less stringent, (and costly), class size and teacher-pupil ratio requirements.

READ MORE FROM WRIGHTSLAW:
"Ethical Burdens" on Psychologists
"School psychologists will increasingly face the burden of deciding whether they work for the schools or for the children."
http://www.wrightslaw.com/advoc/articles/ALESSI1.html

SOLUTION 11:

DISCONTINUE ALLOWING SCHOOLS TO UTILIZE THEIR OWN PERSONNEL TO DIAGNOSE STUDENTS FOR EMOTIONAL OR LEARNING DISABILITIES WHENEVER THE OUTCOMES WILL DIRECTLY AFFECT THE OPERATING BUDGETS OF THE GIVEN SCHOOLS.

12.

REAL PARENTS CARE

America's schools have managed to garner not just legal rights over America's children, but also *legal parental rights,* as was previously mentioned, via the *in loco parentis* clause. In being accorded this right there was most certainly a presumption of equal, if not superior, governmental parenting ability over that of the children's actual parents. But this is faulty thinking. Unlike a government bureaucracy, a good parent actually cares about their child, listens to their child, is attuned to their child's needs, and places the needs of their child above their own, without exception.

Would a good parent seek to cut corners affecting a child's physical health such as declaring catsup a vegetable? (*As was the case in public schools until later overruled by litigation*). Would a good parent isolate a child from needed education for several days for bad behavior? (*Schools do this extensively in the form of "in-school" and "out-of-school" suspensions.*) Would a good parent refuse to give a child a second chance and instead use their mistakes as an opportunity to cite them for failing? (*F still stands for failure.*) Would a good parent of a child with a disability limit the amount of needed services to this child due to cost? Finally, would a good parent **go on strike**?!?

No one has ever studied the effects on students when their teachers, whom many also regard as primary caregivers, choose to publicly and militantly refuse to do their jobs until they are paid more money. If children are affected when their parents argue over money, surely this can't be good for them to see Miss Jones on the 6 o'clock news waving a sign that reads, "I'd rather fight than teach." It also can't be beneficial for their daily routines to be disrupted by such actions, only to return with the illusion of caring teachers now forever shattered. America's schools have become so secure in their positions of superior authority over parents that they have begun usurping parents' rights more and more, even outside of the school arena.

In a much-publicized case of school-related hazing, students who all attended the same high school decided to get together on a Sunday, off school grounds, to commit acts that were at best stupid, and at worst criminal. These students' errors in judgment occurred during a time and place that should have, unarguably, been within their *parents'* jurisdiction. It was not a school-sponsored event, it occurred off school premises, and on a *Sunday*! Nevertheless, seemingly only as a result of bad press, their *school* elected to wield their monopolistic authority over their students' diplomas, (and so their very futures), to punish all involved by ruining their lives, robbing them, forever, from participating in their high school graduations, forever marring the students' end of enduring twelve years of school control. And, why did the school really take such drastic action? Are they planning to punish every subsequent high school student who gets drunk on the weekend and does something stupid? Of course not. These students were punished so severely and with such complete disregard for the rights of their parents in order to deflect their own guilt.

What was apparent early on was the fact that countless teachers, administrators and other school staff were well aware of these students' weekend plans yet not one chose to warn the students' parents. In fact, this "event" had taken place with the school's knowledge year after year without punishment. Now, due to a videotape making its way to the national news, the school suddenly decided to get involved. In "disciplining" the students involved, school authorities were quick to also cite the parents for knowingly permitting their children's participation. Truth be told, it is far less likely that these parents were half as knowledgeable of the event as most school staff. Most parents of 17-year olds are lucky if they can extract more than one-word answers from their kids. Just knowing that the kids were getting together with fellow on a Sunday morning for something even vaguely related to a school sports team would not likely cause most parents to make this their battle of choice. Even the two parents who were apparently coerced by their children to buy beer for the event were undoubtedly aware of the years of community tolerance for this event were probably told that the beer would be poured onto the "hazed" students more than drank. Further, since it was taking place within walking distance of most of the students' homes, none of the kids would be driving, with most returning to the watchful eyes of their parents within the hour. Unfortunately, these students of the class of 2003 were used by their high school as an example to simply protect their own interests.

No amount of teaching students to learn from their mistakes was in play here. The school made absolutely no mea culpa for having known of the event in advance, nor of their having supported it with their silence for decades. Instead, for publicly underscoring the school's bad behavior, the school chose to ruin the kids' lives forever, along with their parents.' They robbed them of one of the most meaningful and momentous events in their children's lives which, when compared to their real parents, they had little to do with occurring in the first place!

READ MORE FROM THE CHICAGO, ILLINOIS SUBURBS:

High School Board Weighs Expulsion of Lacrosse Team Members

http://www.glenviewwatch.com/archive/2004/gw041104.htm

SOLUTION 12:

REDEFINE SCHOOLS ROLE AS "SUBSTITUTE" PARENTS, AND REDIRECT THE EFFORTS TOWARD IMPROVING INSTRUCTION, WHILE ESTABLISHING IMPROVED MEANS FOR STUDENTS TO DEMONSTRATE SUBJECT MASTERY.

13.

SCHOOL PARENTS GET NO RESPECT

For some reason, America's schools have been allowed to become so empowered by their own bureaucracy that most have come to view parents merely as minor annoyances. Regardless of what plaudits of *"Parents as Equal Team Members"* they may espouse in their school mission statements, parents are given next to no decision-making power in school operations whatsoever. Virtually all determinations of instruction, teacher assignments, class placements, school rules, grading standards, discipline policies, extra-curricular priorities, and even the school calendar are decided completely apart from any parental input.

Now, were public school instruction utilized only by the most downtrodden and uneducated families then, perhaps, the logic of this practice might seem more understandable, although still unfair. However, with all but the most elite American's relying on public schools for at least some portion of their children's elementary and secondary schooling, it seems unconscionable that schools should be permitted such broad and unquestioned dictatorship over decisions so greatly affecting so many of our lives. Instead of recognizing parents as their primary benefactors, public school educators too often view parents as pilferers of public resources who must, therefore, be stifled and limited as much as possible when it is actually the other way around. A big part of how schools maintain their power over parents is by professing to have all of the control over our precious children's very futures, and so, *our* futures, as well. This is simply not the case.

Nevertheless, America's schools blatantly usurp parents' rights however it suits their needs, while the majority of parents knowingly let them. Most are too afraid to challenge schools' authority out of a very real fear of retaliation being subtly visited upon their children. Sadly, they quite often are not wrong.

In 2001, an organized school parent-advocacy group marched on the Chicago office of the Illinois State Board of Education (ISBE) where they presented State education officials with over 600 individual parental complaints of misconduct by their children's schools. However, although these complaints were very specific and highly incriminating, *none of their complaints were signed!)* The same parents, so dissatisfied with their children's school performance that they had brought them to this parent advocacy group for help, were too afraid of retaliation by their children's schools against their own children if they were to reveal their identities. Parent fear of school retaliation is a very real threat to school accountability and improvement in America.

Conversely, parents who would express displeasure over a course of their child's medical treatment would unlikely fear a botched surgical procedure by their physician out of spite. This is because, unlike the field of education, the medical profession is bound by a code of ethics placing the life of the patient above all else. Further, if a parent were dissatisfied with their physician they would certainly not be forced by law to stay with this physician. America's schools, however, being accorded the responsibility for perpetuating all knowledge and skills of a society to an entire generation, are held to far lesser accountable. What did ISBE do with the 600 complaints presented to them in good faith, albeit anonymously? Nothing. Rather than show any real consideration for the needs of the students affected by the parents' documented concerns, they, instead, hid behind a statute requiring that all *formal* school complaints be signed, (while concurrently promoting their latest "mission statement," *"Two million children depend on us every day."*) Too bad for them.

Bottom line: *If it's not good enough for the kids in the suburbs then it shouldn't be good enough for kids anywhere in America. Period.*

READ MORE FROM COLUMBIA, MISSOURI:

School board rejects parents' charge of abuse after student was spanked

http://www.columbiatribune.com/2005/Nov/20051120News029.asp

SOLUTION 13:

GIVE SCHOOL PARENTS A VOICE BY REQUIRING STATES TO PUBLISH A PARENT FORUM FOR PARENTS TO EXPRESS THEIR EXPERIENCES AND DISSATISFACTIONS WITH THEIR CHILDREN'S SCHOOLS WITHOUT FEAR OF REPRISAL.

14.

PERPETUATION OF A SOCIAL CASTE SYSTEM

More than any other single aspect of American society, our educational system has the ability to both construct and uphold social divisions based on class, socioeconomic status, and race. It does this largely by allowing grossly substandard education to exist in schools predominated by poor and minority students when compared to schools situated in predominantly "white" upper-income neighborhoods. Almost without exception, the schools at the low end of the opportunity spectrum are the schools producing the lowest scores of student academic achievement. They are also, not coincidentally, the schools with the worst facilities, the fewest resources, and the least-qualified teachers. Now, for years state and local education entities have upheld that these deficits in performance were the students' own making, the result of inadequate and inefficient home conditions, and not due to insufficient or substandard instruction. At the same time, those in positions of power within educational governance have done little or nothing to ensure educational equity within their system.

The famous Brown v. Kansas Board of Education decision was meant to eliminate this disparity. Following this landmark ruling, schools were no longer permitted to segregate students based on race, and were no longer allowed to bar students "of color" from equal educational opportunity. But, *this is exactly what continues to take place today.* The only difference is that it is now being permitted "legally." Unfortunately, by allowing students residing in more affluent neighborhoods to be rewarded with excessive amounts of "private" educational funding, including from area property taxes only creates a "public" system that is highly unbalanced and inequitable.

Currently, state education agencies allow huge disparities in resources to exist between schools within the same sate, county, and even city, which are not entirely the result of differences in community resources. Each state receives a federal flat amount of federal funding this is then distributed to schools by the states. Each school district is then permitted to raise additional funds, in most states via their local property taxes. In addition, there are a number of state and federal grants for which schools and districts can apply, along with the possibility of municipal bonds in some cases. (There is also much money to be gained via athletics, concessions, fundraisers, and so on.)

The No Child Left Behind Act was supposedly designed to protect students from enduring inadequate instruction and facilities, particularly if these schools produced evidence of consistently substandard student achievement. According to this new federal mandate, rather than continue to be subjected to these failures, parents were to be offered the choice of sending their children to another school. Unfortunately, most American schools almost immediately seized upon a loophole in this law by quickly applying their own structure to this "*choice*" option. As though they had the right, many American schools developed significant parameters, often limiting parental school choice to only one or two schools of the districts' choosing. In Chicago, during the first phase of NCLB "choice," parents of students from five schools found to be substandard were provided only one alternative school within the district of over 600. At no time were these parents given the choice of relocating their children to any of the district's truly superior schools, nor were parents provided the truth about the disparity in distribution of school district resources, services or talent. So long as the wording of this law remains unchanged, they never will.

READ MORE FROM SAN FRANCISCO, CALIFORNIA:

**Study cites divide for rich, poor kids
Big inequities seen in Bay Area**

http://www.sfgate.com/cgi-bin/article.cgi?f=/chronicle/archive/2001/11/28/MN125858.DTL

SOLUTION 14:

HOLD ALL SCHOOL INSTRUCTION, STAFFING, AND BUILDINGS TO THE SAME STANDARDS. IF IT'S NOT GOOD ENOUGH FOR THE KIDS IN THE SUBURBS, THEN IT SHOULDN'T BE GOOD ENOUGH FOR KIDS ANYWHERE. PERIOD. NO CHILDREN IN AMERICA SHOULD BE FORCED TO ATTEND ANY SCHOOL WITH LESS TO OFFER THAN ANY OTHER SCHOOL IN AMERICA AND NO PARENT SHOULD BE FORCED TO SEND THEM THERE.

15.

NEIGHBORHOOD SCHOOLS – OK FOR *GOOD* NEIGHBORHOODS

One of the major constructs of modern American life is the neighborhood school. It has become a symbol of our local identities, our values, and our pride. Realtors nationwide, when using the premise, "Location, location, location," to describing market values, almost always place the quality of the local schools above all else in determining the relative worth of an area.

And, although collective lifestyles have changed significantly since America moved from the one-room country school to the local elementary, middle, and high school format in the early 50's, the neighborhood school has remained one of the few bastions of stability in our otherwise evolving society. In some American locales this may still works just fine. In others, however, the local schools do little to contribute positively to the futures of America's youth, while some appear even to be doing more harm than good.

The reality is this: Schools in bad neighborhoods will never be fully staffed by the most desirable teachers, at long as America continues to have a significant teacher shortage. Given the choice, most teachers will always opt for the more lucrative conditions and salaries in the more desirable neighborhoods. Yet, at the same time, many of the America's brightest and most talented physicians are employed by large teaching hospitals frequently located in some of the most blighted urban areas. Why? Because these facilities have been developed and promoted as offering superior challenges not afforded physicians working in areas experiencing little crime or tragedy. Unlike the education field, the medical field prides itself on being able to meet its most difficult challenges in these superior, but undesirably located, facilities, while their staff pride themselves on the superior skill required to succeed in these settings. Of course, these facilities also offer their professionals superior compensation.

While there is, unarguably, a definite need for de-centralized neighborhood social centers, such as recreational facilities, in neighborhoods with high-crime statistics, these are able to be staffed by non-degreed, often minimum-wage earning or volunteer coaches and others, frequently from the neighborhoods themselves. Unfortunately, most highly-skilled and educated teachers are able to find teaching jobs without risking their lives to do so.

Bottom line: *If some American schools are situated in neighborhoods considered so wretched and dangerous that they could never maintain safe conditions or attract qualified instructors, then what are we doing sending our children there?*

**READ MORE FROM THE
ANNIE E. CASEY FOUNDATION:**

"Although poor neighborhoods include individuals and families with extraordinary resilience and strength, too many kids growing up in such environments will reach adulthood unprepared to parent, to work, and to contribute to society."

http://www.aecf.org/kidscount/kc1997/overview.htm

SOLUTION 15:

WHEN NECESSARY CERTAIN STUDENTS MAY NEED TO BE TRANSPORTED TO ATTEND MORE CENTRALIZED, SAFER, STATE OF THE ART SCHOOLS WHERE THEY MAY RECEIVE INSTRUCTION FROM SUPERIORALLY-TALENTED AND COMPENSATED TEACHERS.

16.

SO, WHAT'S THE REAL POINT OF SCHOOL?

Okay, so the current school system isn't perfect, but at least it does what it's supposed to do right? Well, that depends. If parents believe their local school is simply supposed to prepare their children to be knowledgeable of everything but great at nothing, then the current system might work for them. But, except for a very few American parents whose children were all blessed with superior intelligence allowing them to be successful at everything they do with or without their school's help, most parents of American school children have experienced at least some degree of frustration with the seemingly uncaring "one size fits all" approach to instruction that is crammed into a typical school day.

Several major philosophies co-exist related to whether schools should exist primarily to prepare students for self-sustaining careers, for responsible citizenship, or simply for the sake of learning itself without any particular long-range goals. However, most parents would like to think that by the time their child completes 12 years of compulsory education they will at least be prepared for a job *interview*, if not a job. With this in mind, there are a handful of subjects most American's seem to agree are the most necessary for children's intellectual development. Little did our forefathers know, however, that these *"three R's,"* once deemed the primary, if not the only, elements of a basic education of America's future adults, now have been heavily interspersed with sewing, swimming, softball, square dancing, and shop. Today, due largely to America's two very powerful teachers' unions, (the NEA and the AFT), *all* school subjects, regardless of their relative value to advancing American society, must now be accorded equal time in schools. This is because all American teachers, regardless of subject matter, are considered to be entitled to equal pay and an equitable teaching schedule. So, regardless of whether certain students require additional time to grasp certain reading, writing, or math skills, they are, instead, shuffled off to learn to make Jell-O®, do the backstroke, or the do-se-do, to comply with the teaching (not learning) schedule.

In the early 1960's two major movements were initiated in America's schools. One, driven by a national obsession with failing to be the first world power to put a man into space, and the other from the President's concern for his citizens' physical health. These movements resulted in greater emphasis on advanced science and math instruction, coupled with mandatory physical fitness classes for all students throughout their school career. This led to a surge of new teachers whose only certification or training is in "Physical" Education, meaning they were only qualified to teach softball, volleyball, tennis, badminton, and other similar "pastimes." Now while these are all honorable pursuits imparting the values of teamwork and sportsmanship, parents can, and often do, utilize non-certified recreational personnel at far less cost to provide very similar instructing to their children. Schools were originally established to provide instruction to America's children *that they could not likely acquire elsewhere.* There are countless recreational and community programs and staff members capable of providing much of this non-academic instruction, for which public schools have now established an overwhelming, and costly monopoly.

Considering that most of America's schools are struggling to afford enough qualified staff to meet all of its students' basic *academic* needs, it seems ludicrous, if not fiscally foolish, to waste education dollars or time on instructors whose entire high five- and six-figure salaries pays for instruction that has no bearing on improving a students' knowledge or skills in reading, writing, mathematics, history, foreign languages, nor any of the sciences. Currently, teachers of calculus, biochemistry, and Latin do not earn a penny more than those teaching "Freshman P.E." (Actually, many earn less, since most P.E. teachers also earn plumb extra stipends for coaching sports teams.)

READ MORE FROM JOHN STOSSEL:

"Stupid in America -
Why your kids are probably dumber than Belgians"

http://www.reason.com/hod/js011306.shtml

SOLUTION 16:

ELIMINATE THE PRACTICE OF SCHOOLS BEING OBLIGATED TO DO MORE THAN PROVIDE STUDENTS A QUALITY ACADEMIC EDUCATION BY FORGOING MANY OF THEIR NON-EDUCATIONAL RESPONSIBILITIES AND DEFERRRING LESS CRITICAL DISCIPLINES TO OTHER MORE WELL-SUITED ORGANIZATIONS, (WHICH WOULD ALSO CREATE MORE NEEDED NON-DEGREED JOBS.

17.

ATHLETIC v. ACADEMIC ACHIEVEMENT

America's schools' primary mission is to impart a core set of knowledge and skills required for its students to qualify for college and gainful employment, why, then, are students' individual achievement in these areas kept hidden, while their athletic achievements are published each week in the local paper? The ability to acquire knowledge and to meet academic requirements is largely within most students' grasp, while physical stamina and coordination are primarily the result of genetics. Nevertheless, it is the ability to throw or catch a ball or run a race that is recognized as a symbol of school and community pride, while the ability to reach superior mathematical, science, or writing scores is kept hidden, or at least only referenced in vague terms, such as "national merit scholar," rather than with specific statistics, as with sports

Could there be a more clear illustration of our national priorities? Of course, this message is not lost on our youth who celebrate the "C" student who can make the tackle, but shun the "A" student who refuses to participate in the "senior prank." At a relatively small handful of schools in this country, their students' superior test scores ensure a continued rise in local property values. However, for the majority of America's schools, it is their sports teams that are the real "big business" in the community generating the big revenues, revenues that many schools can ill-afford to do without.

There appears to be a misperception that, with tenacity and diligence, all athletic shortcomings can be overcome, while one's academic potential is far more limited. In fact, in most cases, the reverse that is actually true. Nevertheless, using this faulty logic, one's academic performance is often viewed more as a sense of failure than of shame, and so considered to be subject to "confidentiality" provisions equal to that of medical records. Until American's schools begin to recognize and celebrate academic accomplishments over non-academic ones, school achievement will never truly be regarded as a priority by most of its students.

READ MORE FROM *USA TODAY*:

"Half of teens say school's unsafe"

http://www.usatoday.com/news/education/2005-08-16-school-safety_x.htm

---

SOLUTION 17:

REDUCE SCHOOL AWARDS FOR **PHYSICAL ACHIEVEMENTS** *WHILE INCREASING THEM FOR* **ACADEMIC** *ACCOMPLISHMENTS. INCREASE ACCOLADES FOR MATH, SCIENCE, WRITING, AND PUBLIC SPEAKING. DEVELOP AMERICAN SCHOOLS' IDENTITY BASED ON PRIDE IN LEARNING AND ACHIEVEMENT, WHILE CELEBRATING* **ACADEMIC "STARS."**

THE FORMAT

"WHAT'S GOING ON HERE?"

18.

**TOO MUCH TO HANDLE,
(WELL, THAT IS)**

Once upon a time the very concept of "school" in America literally meant the opportunity to spend eight years, (if you were lucky), in one multi-age classroom being drilled in the "3 R's" until sufficiently and sequentially mastered, and that's it! Even until as recently as the early 1960's, students were afforded little in the way of extra-curricular activities or services by their schools. Of course, back then, parents were still expected to do the bulk of the child rearing. School priorities were more focused on each child learning their times tables, perfecting the Palmer Method, and being able to read the entire "Dick and Jane" series. Schools today, however, are a very different animal. Not only are these institutions expected to teach students to read and write and do math, they are expected to meet all of their social, emotional, athletic, vocational, musical, artistic, and medical needs, as well.

A very small percentage of America's schools actually manage to accomplish this fairly well. Naturally, they are situated in America's wealthiest regions, while also serving America's brightest youth, those in need of their schools' state of the art services the least. Meanwhile, as more and more of America's remaining school systems are now producing horrendous student achievement scores, it only stands to reason that they could better reach their required *mandatory* learning benchmarks if they lightened their load of some of their less-critical responsibilities. Instead, too many schools in America are attempting to accomplish far more than is either reasonable or necessary. One glaring example among many is "Physical Education." This is not to suggest that America's youth should all suddenly become even more sedentary than they already are. However, if, as is true in many schools, football practice, junior officer training, and Driver's Education may be substituted for P.E., then why not private outside ballet class, karate, or gymnastics classes, or any of a plethora of other available outside recreational activities? A significant number of parents are already paying for these and countless other opportunities for physical activity. Why, then, should their children's schools consume any of the rest of their kids' day with more "recreational" pursuits at the expense of academic learning? Those who cannot afford these after-school classes could participate in any number of comparable community-sponsored programs. Most schools already provide some amount of after-school programming to its students.

While serving to break schools' monopoly on these non-academic pursuits and creating more non-degreed jobs, (to the benefit of many communities), this plan would also free up schools, and their college-educated instructors, for more necessary education. Of course, most schools would never go for this suggestion willingly, since much of their identity, not to mention their revenues, are dependent upon their sports teams, an extension of the P.E. departments.

A recent report of New York City schools indicates 10,000 3rd graders failed to meet minimum academic standards, and they are not alone. America's schools are doing far too many things poorly to do their main job well any longer. The standardized assessments of school achievement test in only four areas: Reading, Math, Writing, and Science. While History should probably be included, anything else is beyond the scope of what is deemed of primary importance with schools, and should be regarded as such.

> **READ MORE FROM CHARLOTTE, NORTH CAROLINA:**
>
> "**Why Block Scheduling:**
>
> *"Fragmented Instruction, Impersonal, factory like environments, Discipline problems are caused by too many distractions, Instructional Possibilities are limited, Traditional scheduling prohibits varying learning time for students."*
>
> http://coe.winthrop.edu/vawterd/block/why.html

SOLUTION 18:

LET THE SCHOOLS' PARENTS DECIDE HOW THEIR SCHOOLS' EXTRA-CURRICULAR MONIES ARE SPENT!

19.

ONE SIZE FITS SOME

One of the difficulties with any organization seeking to accomplish one set of goals for an entire group is that, in most cases, the success rates of some will be far greater success than others. From their first day of school students are plugged into "grade levels" with other students with whom they share the same September 1 to August 31 twelve-month year of birth, but who likely do not share their same levels of intellect or skill development. Nevertheless, regardless of individual strengths or weaknesses, all students are held to this arbitrary standard as the defining measure of their expected level of achievement, understanding, and cognitive growth. Students who happen to develop ahead or behind their same-aged peers, or, God forbid, *inconsistently* from the norm in different academic disciplines, will have little chance of attaining their schools' official definition of academic excellence. For those whose brains happened to develop faster than average, much of the "age appropriate" instruction of their prescribed "grade level" is far too slow-paced and boring, leading them to develop patterns of apathy and under achievement. Those who lag behind, often due to being born at the "young" end of the grade year, are almost never recognized for actually making an appropriate level of academic growth for their age.

What would make far more sense would be for America's schools to group its students by *mastery levels*. While this concept has sometimes been equated with "retention," or "holding back" students who fail to meet minimal learning standards, this one drawback could easily be overcome by simply placing all students of a particular age range into subject-matter instructional groups with other students who share the same or similar level of academic achievement. This way, students performing ahead of their peers in Math but behind them in Reading could receive instruction in both disciplines at levels most appropriate to their particular levels of academic development.

Now, while requirements for school instruction are becoming ever more standardized, the levels of mastery can be more easily tied to students' performance on state and federal tests of student achievement. Currently, these tests are treated merely as an extra added burden by most American schools, with students being offered no incentive to complete them to their maximum potential. If students' performance on these exams were to suddenly be considered mandatory for their promotion to the next grade level, *(or level of mastery),* or if teachers were required to produce prescribed increases in student achievement on these exams from year to year, both America's student and teacher performance would likely improve greatly.

READ MORE FROM BOSTON, MASSACHUSETTS:

One-Size-Fits-All Education Doesn't Work

http://www.alfiekohn.org/teaching/onesize.htm

AND

FROM CONNECTICUT:

Do Schools Give 'Equal Grades for Equal Work'?

http://www.educationworld.com/a_issues/issues105.shtml

AND

FROM SEATTLE, WASHINGTON:

"Going Beyond Social Promotion"

http://www.topschools.com/Retention.htm

SOLUTION 19:

REPLACE "GRADE-LEVELS" WITH "MASTERY-LEVELS" WHILE DIVIDING EACH SUBJECT INTO STAGES OF LEARNING WITH OPPORTUNITIES FOR DOCUMENTED MASTERY PRIOR TO STUDENTS PROGRESSING TO THE NEXT LEVEL OF INSTRUCTION, WITH THEIR PROGRESSION BEING BASED ON ACTUAL DEMONSTRATED STUDENT PERFORMANCE – NOT AN ARTIFICIAL AND MEANINGLESS TIMELINE.

20.

TOO MANY CHANGES

When was the last time you spent the day, either at work or at home, switching from one project to the next, every 45 minutes, from morning until late afternoon? Sure, there may have been that one day you started cleaning the garage and then realized you needed to do some yard work, which led to fixing that broken rake, which led to doing some laundry, which led to writing that grocery list. But did you actually accomplish anything? Barely. Could you work that way every day? No way. Not toward the achievement anything really important, that is.

However, this is precisely the schedule to America's schools expect our kids to adhere for 12 years! Some learn to adapt. Others never do. This means of compartmentalized learning is not a natural tendency handed down by our forefathers. For many students, this teacher-convenient schedule has driven thousands of students up the wall, literally! Knowing that ADD and ADHD are not proven diseases but merely a compilation of identifiable symptoms, some have come to believe that schools actually *cause* these conditions by expecting more of our children than what is physically or intellectually possible for a good number of them.

While these hourly changes are not always so obvious in the elementary grades, by "middle school," (which, due to overcrowding, seems to occur at increasingly earlier grade levels), students are expected to adapt to this hourly subject-switching format with ease. Unfortunately, for many students, it takes them at least half an hour for them to reorient their brains to new forms of learning and thinking. For others, knowing that this change is only temporary, they are simply unable to commit themselves sufficiently to a given topic. Few adults, as well, would ever attempt to tackle a major learning task in less than an hour, particularly knowing that they would be expected to move on to a series of new and unrelated subjects immediately thereafter.

At the high school level, in particular, these transitions are in place primarily to satisfy union rules, not student needs. Because, according to collective bargaining agreements, all teachers, regardless of subject area, are accorded equal instructional time with equal pay-scales, this naturally leads to sewing teachers and calculus teachers being accorded with equal status and educational value, at least in the schools' practice, if not in actual administrative belief. With America's schools being held increasingly more accountable for the achievement of their students in core academic areas, one would anticipate a shift in how schools prioritize their use of time and teacher compensation. Unfortunately, the current system is so deeply entrenched in the schools' structure and staff expectations that most administrators feel powerless to defy the status quo, regardless of the resulting negative outcomes to their schools or their students.

READ MORE FROM
ILLINOIS STATE UNIVERSITY:
WHAT ARE OUR SCHOOLS TRYING TO DO?
http://www.wiman.us/schoolsdoitall.html

SOLUTION 20:

MAKE INSTRUCTION MORE STUDENT-ACCESSIBLE AND STOP REQUIRING ALL STUDENTS TO MEET MULTIPLE ACADEMIC EXPECATIONS EACH DAY.

21.

DISCIPLINE = VACATION
(Or TEACHERS ARE NOT THE POLICE)

For a variety of reasons, a significant percentage of students display what many teachers deem less-than-acceptable behaviors when made to endure endless days sitting in the same assigned seats in rooms that rarely change, where almost nothing exciting ever happens, day after day, after year after year. While federal and state learning goals contain absolutely no requirements with regard to either rewarding or penalizing students' behavior, schools have, nevertheless, made it their first priority to "train" students to all behave in a certain way, while often withholding instruction and passing grades for a laundry list of misdeeds inconsequential to the students' academic performance. Now, naturally, schools must make it their business to keep their facilities safe, meaning any truly serious offenses such as those involving the use or possession of weapons, guns, or drugs must be dealt with accordingly. However, these are matters best handled by the police, relieving schools of the responsibility for imposing dual or substitute sanctions. Meanwhile, for the far more frequent instances of less serious student offenses such as "talking out of turn," "leaving one's seat," or "not having a pencil," schools could do well to simply overlook most of these petty infractions, while realizing students are still individuals with very human qualities and needs.

Wait, you say, such lackadaisical controls would lead to complete anarchy! Total chaos would ensue and students would simply stop learning altogether! To the contrary, by perpetuating a series of power struggles rooted primarily in crowd control, student learning and motivation already suffer significantly. To presume that by leaving students to their own devices that most students would cease to have an interest in learning indicates a complete lack of confidence in both one's ability to teach and in the viability of one's given subject matter. America's schools spend an inordinate amount of time and manpower penalizing students for what are deemed unacceptable actions. The most widely utilized student penalty, while also having the least relationship to logical consequences, is the practice of preventing those students who have failed, through their misbehaviors, to demonstrate significant interest in attending school, *from attending classes for an extended period of time!* This practice, known both as the "in-school" and "out-of school suspension" typically means retaining students throughout a school day or a series of days either in a room devoid of any instruction, while typically managed by non-certified staff, or simply preventing students from attending school at all. Few students, once having developed poor attitudes toward school, (characterized by a lack of preparation, appropriateness, or timeliness), fail to realize that by simply continuing their undesirable behaviors they are almost guaranteeing themselves a "vacation" from the state-mandated drudgery that even their own parents can do little to prevent.

    Finally, students who fail to adhere to strict standards of behavior, but who can otherwise demonstrate sufficient acquisition of the prescribed instruction, are, nevertheless, most often given "lowered grades" that are more based on their behavior, than their learning. Here's an example: A child with above average ability in the area of reading and writing finds the many of the required English assignments dull and boring, but who still manages to submit them all in superior form just prior to the end of the term, risks being penalized with a significantly lowered grade, based solely on timing. This is true even if these assignments reflect a level of learning that is far superior to those of the other students. Although "letter grades," which are simply too subjective to be assigned so much life-determining power, are intended to be based on a student's level of mastery, (e.g. "A" reflecting at least a 90% mastery level, "B" at least an 80%, etc.). Instead, too often these indicators are altered for non-mastery reasons as a means of punishment for students failing to comply with various arbitrary teacher rules. This is neither academically indicated nor fiscally ethical. Students' very lives are being compromised by power-driven school personnel who are being permitted to make continual and arbitrary judgments over students' very lives, not due to a lack of intelligence or achievement, but simply because they refuse to conform.

READ MORE FROM PITTSBURGH, PENNSYLVANIA:

"Teachers not lords of discipline"

http://www.pittsburghlive.com/x/pittsburghtrib/s_184451.html

SOLUTION 21:

STOP DENYING STUDENTS AN EDUCATION SIMPLY FOR FAILING TO COMPLY WITH ARBITRARY RULES HAVING LITTLE OR NOTHING TO DO WITH LEARNING.

22.

SCHOOL SCHEDULES: A BURDEN ON THE PARENTS

It's a few years now into the 21st Century, when the overwhelming majority of America's schoolchildren reside in households where all parents also living in the home work at least part-time. This means, with few exceptions, the parents are leaving the house each weekday morning as early as their children, if not earlier, with almost as many not returning until 5 p.m. or later. Despite the passage of the Family Leave Act of the 1990's, most employer's personnel policies have restricted the application of this act to specific, pre-arranged circumstances, and not simply because their employees' children's schools are having a half-day for the "Taffy Apple Sale," or another inconvenient reason.

Even America's regular school day schedules are far from convenient for most American parents, and haven't been so for at least 25 years, yet nothing has been done to try to change this fact. Most American schools, which supposedly exist to serve America's families, still maintain a schedule that was designed in the 1940's, based on the needs of families of that era, when mothers stayed at home and cooked and cleaned all day, and then welcomed their children home mid-afternoon to help them with their homework, serving them an early supper before their hard-working fathers walked in the door at 6:30, just in time to kiss their children goodnight. Back then, there was simply no need for school to be extended until 4 or 5 p.m. Today, however, this results in the majority of America's kids either going home to an empty house or moving directly from school to an after school daycare arrangement.

"Latchkey" kids, an unfortunate new word coined in the 1970's to describe the growing number of kids going home from school each day to an empty house and not adult supervision, has had little impact on schools' scheduling policies.

The primary reason for school's continued adherence to their "parent-unfriendly" schedules is the teachers' unions. Because teachers' salaries are negotiated based on a prescribed number of "instructional hours" per day, for a set number of days per year, any move toward increasing their workdays schedule by another two hours, to coincide with the hours of most other comparable jobs, would result in their being entitled to significant and cost-prohibitive salary increases. To meet parents' needs to have their children remain at school beyond 3 o'clock, many schools have added after school daycare programs that consist largely of non-educational custodial care only, staffed by non-union, non-certified staff.

Meanwhile, as growing numbers of America's schools continue to fail to adequately educate their students within their current time schedules, (as evidenced by achievement test scores), there are far more sensible solutions to their use of time. In most middle and upper class neighborhoods parents pay for their children to participate in a number of supplementary activities and learning opportunities, even though these mean even more time away from home beyond the school and after school program hours. Much of the students' schooldays are filled with pursuits that are significant departures for the core curricula. What would seem to make sense would be for the hours from 8 until 3 to be devoted exclusively to Reading, Writing, Mathematics, History, and Science, (the only subjects on which a school's instructional performance is based), with the hours from 3 until 5 being those devoted to art, sports, music, drama, crafts, dance, singing, as well as any other non-academic pursuits for which the school already employs teachers, but for which other non-certified professionals could also be utilized to meet these students' needs more economically. This way, schools would not need to extend their academic day or year, but could provide the types of supplemental coursework that makes their education more "well-rounded," while also increasing student academic instructional time and, at the same time, meeting a significant parental need.

READ MORE FROM THE WASHINGTON POST:

"Abandoning after-school: Bush says one thing, does another for America's working parents."

http://www.workingforchange.com/article.cfm?itemid=14615

SOLUTION 22:

KEEP SCHOOLS OPEN YEAR-ROUND WHILE DISCONTINUING THE PRACTICE OF IMPOSITING STATE CONTROLS ON PARENTS' INDIVIDUAL FREEDOMS. ALLOW PARENTS THE AUTHORITY TO PLAN THEIR FAMILIES' VACATION AND LEISURE TIME WITHOUT BEING SUBJECT TO LEGAL SANCTIONS. MAKE SCHOOLS MORE FLEXIBLE BY PROVIDING STUDENTS MISSED LESSONS. RELAX TRUANCY STANDARDS TO MERELY REQUIRING A CERTAIN AMOUNT OF ATTENDANCE DAYS WITHIN ANY 12-MONTH YEAR.

23.

SCHOOLS' *"PRISON MENTALITY"*

One of the greatest indicator of the success or failure of America's schools is its impact on the future viability of its youth. Countless studies have shown that adults tend to gravitate toward that which is familiar from their childhoods. We sentence our children to 12+ years of a life that is largely institutionalized, lacking in emotion or individual expression. In the relatively few schools in "good" neighborhoods, this is largely disguised by beautiful surroundings, shiny new textbooks, and smiling teachers. Not so, however, for a growing number of schools struggling just to keep the building heated.

In schools with limited resources what is also often absent is any sense of a supportive or nurturing learning environment. Instead of making the students feel encouraged and welcomed, many of America's poorer schools are run more like prisons than learning centers. Coupled with the lack of instructional resources, including bathrooms with no privacy stalls, water fountains with brown water, mice, cockroaches, ceilings dripping with God knows what, broken glass littering the playgrounds, and poorly-lit windowless classrooms, their school hallways are typically staffed with a number individuals of questionable background, often seemingly not unlike common thugs, employed like "bouncers" to maintain crowd control. Students in these schools are frequently treated as criminals, for the minor infractions and regardless of innocence or guilt. Often it is these untrained "professionals" who are accorded much of the responsibility for issuing student consequences. There is a pervasive culture of fear, with those of greatest connections to power or physical strength ruling over those with less.

Passing through metal detectors and/or being frisked on a daily basis is another common experience now shared by the majority of American high school students, only underscoring a presumption of guilt and distrust. Despite acts of violence that periodically occur in other public settings, most Americans are able to come and go from their jobs without such intense scrutiny. Those who *do* undergo such daily screenings do so *by choice,* not by law. America should be deeply concerned by the mindset being imposed on so many of its young adults who are being subjected to a daily dose of life based on a *"Do as I say or pay"* mentality, while also being accorded almost no opportunity for self-direction or individual expression. There is a very real chance that too many will develop an unhealthy dependency on this level of authority that will eventually bring them back to the only lifestyle that feels familiar to them, America's penitentiaries.

READ MORE FROM
THE FUTURE OF FREEDOM FOUNDATION:
Public Schools: Turning Children and Parents into Peons

http://www.fff.org/freedom/0797d.asp
AND

FROM THE
CALIFORNIA TEACHERS' ASSOCIATION:

Where everybody knows your name
-- Can smaller schools give students an edge?
http://www.cta.org/CaliforniaEducator/v6i3/feature_smaller.htm

---

SOLUTION 23:

ELIMINATE SCHOOLS' FOCUS ON CROWD CONTROL WITH STUDENTS BEING TREATED AS INMATES, BY ESTABLISHING SMALLER ENROLLMENTS WITH REDUCED STUDENT-TEACHER RATIOS.

24.

UNREALISTIC CLASS SIZES

When was the last time you tried to really teach anyone anything? Now, how about a group of people? Most parents can recall at least one or two experiences leading a Brownie troop, Cub Scout pack, or Sunday school class. Managing 15 or 20 kids was one thing, but teaching them each something was another, right? It usually required that the steps or information was mapped out in advance and well-planned. Of course, this is the *job* of most classroom teachers, a job they *chose*. However, imagine for a moment being required to teach approximately 28 students, all at different levels of understanding and motivation a series of prescribed lessons, often on a variety of subjects, for 5 to 6 hours per day, 5 days per week!

It's really not as easy as it sounds. Teachers today often bear the brunt of the criticism when a student fails to learn. What no one stops to consider is the large number of students whom teachers are generally required to instruct at one time, and all during a given school year. Further, what is also often overlooked is the enormous number of non-teaching responsibilities to which many teachers must also adhere. This includes maintaining grade books, lesson plans, attendance logs, professional development hours, and assignment grading. Special education teachers often have fewer students, but about five times the additional paperwork, coupled with an array of students having a far more disparate set of abilities and special needs.

Is it no wonder, then, that teachers have resorted to merely "presenting" in most cases, relying heavily on students' (and parents') own initiative to absorb any material requiring additional time or explanation? Teacher training devotes almost no time to how to meet the multiple demands of a teaching job. It often presumes a setting that is devoid of deadlines or bell schedules. Present class size maximums are not designed to adequately meet the needs of all students, only those with average to slightly above-average abilities. Those who could do just fine with simply a little more repetition or slower pace are either relegated to "special education" classes or awarded a failing grade. More advanced and gifted students often suffer, as well, by being made to endure instruction that is far below their abilities, also contributing to their poor performance.

As long as schools continue to rely on large-group instructional models (and anything over 5 or 6 kids *is* large, (remember the Cub Scouts?), they will continue to serve only the student in the middle, while the instructional needs of those at either end are simply sacrificed on their behalf, penalizing both the confused and the bored in the name of *"Classroom Management."*

READ MORE FROM CALIFORNIA:
As budgets shrink, class sizes expand

http://www.csmonitor.com/2003/0311/p01s01-usgn.html

SOLUTION 24:

PROVIDE STUDENTS MORE OPPORTUNITIES FOR SELF-DIRECTED LEARNING AND WHILE REDUCING THE BURDEN ON TEACHERS TO ACTUALLY "TEACH" 25 TO 30 STUDENTS AT ONE TIME.

25.

DISCRETIONARY FUNDS & UNEQUAL GRANTS

Anyone who believes that the discrepancy in education funding is the result the "haves" naturally reaping more than the "have nots" is not fully aware of the "big picture." Sometimes, in addition to property tax disparities, there are other forces at work furthering this inequity, as well. One highly politicized school funding source is state grants. Each state is able to award grants for computer equipment, new construction, art programs, "safe school" programs, and countless other special interests at the discretion of state education administrators. Oftentimes the poorer schools are denied equal access to these resources simply because they fail to employ a full-time grant writer. The majority of these state grants are awarded based on a "contest" of sorts, with funding going to the schools with the well-worded applications.

As a result, schools already enjoying some of the most lucrative education budgets are able to procure additional state grants for such lavish items as $2 million dollars worth of security cameras in every alcove, $200,000 for a darkroom, or $20,000 for show choir costumes, while other schools in the same county are lacking even working computers or sprinklers.

Within many of America's schools that are "flush" with sufficient funding, it is also not unusual for new musical instruments, sports equipment, utility vehicles, office décor, and much more to be ordered by individual departments without any required accountability to their stakeholders. Frequently there is an attitude of "use it or lose it," with department heads in many schools scrambling to order sufficient equipment, materials, or supplies, regardless of need, so as to ensure that no amount of their budgets will be reallocated, albeit to more needy programs, the following year.

Surely there are parents who have long resented their tax dollars going to pay for equipment and materials for a number of extracurricular programs for which their own children do not take part, or *worse,* for those their kids sought to participate but were turned down due to unnecessarily rigorous "tryouts." (Is it really that important to deny any students the chance to participate in drill team who *want* to participate?)

While state grants should be awarded based on need, they are, instead, often awarded based on well-articulated greed. Public school expenditures should be limited to those approved by the majority of a school's parents, not by just an elite few. Further, *all* expenditures should be made very clear to all stakeholders prior to any proposed school tax increases.

**READ MORE FROM THE
HAWAII DEPARTMENT OF EDUCATION:**

A Review of the Incentive and Innovation Grant Review Panel of the Department of Education

http://www.hawaii.gov/auditor/Overviews/1994/94-24.htm

SOLUTION 25:

A SCHOOL'S **ENTIRE** *BUDGET SHOULD BE CLEARLY ARTICULATED TO ALL WHO ARE AFFECTED BY ITS SPENDING DECISIONS.*

26.

DEPARTMENTAL COMPETITION = PERFORMANCE ISOLATION

One of the biggest misconceptions of those outside the field of education regarding the operation of America's schools concerns the extent of communication between various school professionals and departments. While most might presume that teachers who share students would communicate periodically regarding their strengths, weaknesses, learning styles, and special circumstances, this almost never occurs. Further, most instructional decision-making, as well, takes place along parallel, non-intersecting tracts, even when collaboration would save both resources and time.

For the most part, teachers in one grade level or subject area exist in a vacuum, with little meaningful interaction with other teachers or departments. This is just one more condition of American education that is borne out of a structure based more on equal time and equal pay for teachers than what is actually best for their students. Teachers actually bear little responsibility for their students once the kids are promoted out of their classes. Almost no feedback regarding students' subsequent performance is shared with their prior instructors, including which concepts were retained and which one's had to be re-taught; which teaching methods worked and which failed miserably. Consequently, teachers could conceivably be instructing poorly in one or more areas without any expectation of responsibility or accountability. Even students' standardized achievement test scores are not usually learned until the following school year, and so are only provided to their *current* teachers, not those responsible for providing the applicable instruction at the time they were tested.

Another counterproductive aspect of most of America's schools' internal structures is how each department, be it "early childhood," "elementary reading," "middle school science," or "high school athletics," is governed by its own separate leadership, with separate priorities, competing for a slice of the same budget pie. There is little that is shared between departments regarding individual students' learning needs, only matters related to school operations. Almost every department chair, coordinator, and supervisor is permitted to establish their own policies regarding instruction, grading, and expenditures, with little any concern for what is best for the students or the school as a whole.

In many cases, teachers are encouraged to spend the entire amount they have been accorded for materials and supplies or else risk this amount being reduced the following year. Consequently, while some departments are struggling to afford enough textbooks for every student, others are purchasing additional band instruments, art supplies, and computer software, simply to "use up" their budgets.

State departments of education must begin requiring schools to utilize standardized tests with faster turn around times, while establishing greater correlations between test scores and teacher performance, as well as instructional expenditures. Currently, students' test scores are barely even considered in any of the day-to-day instruction. Further, individual teachers are simply not held accountable for the performance of their students, nor compared with the scores of students' from different teachers. While states compile elaborate "school report cards" displaying data related to schools' overall school performance, no comparison of individual teacher outcomes is included. Although this data that is readily available, is not even extrapolated or considered.

In no other industry or profession is so little relationship drawn between performance and outcomes. It is as though teacher performance is meant to have minimal, if any, bearing on student academic achievement. In what other industry are there an *expected* percentage of failures? Where else, in fact, is a *lack* of failures is considered suspect? Where else are failures not attributed to the professionals? Until teachers are actually expected to successfully teach *all* students, when responsibility for students' "F's" are shared by students and teachers alike, this phenomena of "guilt-free teaching" will likely continue. Only when it serves their needs will teachers finally become motivated toward greater utilization and sharing of teaching methods and practices that actually work.

READ MORE FROM HARVARD UNIVERSITY:

Why the Teacher Crisis Is Worse Than You Think (and What Can Be Done About It)

http://www.gse.harvard.edu/news/features/boles060120 03.html

SOLUTION 26:

MEASURE BOTH TEACHERS' AND SCHOOL DEPARTMENTS' PERFORMANCE BY THE ACADEMIC GROWTH OF THEIR STUDENTS, WHILE REQUIRING THAT SCHOOL RESOURCES BE MORE STANDARDIZED TO MINIMIZE FISCAL ABUSE.

27.

NEGATIVE PRESSURES OF SCHOOL ON *"MISFITS"*

First and foremost, America sends its children to school for an education. That is, to learn the academic subjects that parents and ordinary citizens are unable to teach them. Secondary to this purpose, in most cases, are all of the socialization benefits to the kids, which are derived from participating in group activities with their peers. However, inherent in this expectation is that *all* students will be given an equal opportunity to participate and to belong. Unfortunately, this is rarely the case. There exists in America's schools a pervasive attitude against anything that is outside of the status quo. For students who fail their schools' ideal, school socialization is anything but beneficial, and is, in fact, often sheer torture.

For one thing, despite all of the recent legislation meant to support the needs of students with disabilities, the majority of these students are still isolated from their peers, either physically or psychologically, via labels, separate curriculum, or other obvious distinctions. Students with other differences in height, weight, hair length, or even attire, rarely realize sufficient representation, inclusion, or equality.

By high school, gay students already know the pain of failing to fit the norm personified by the homecoming queen and king. Students lacking in athletic ability are continually held in lesser status than those who do, while those with any language limitations, family or economic difficulties, or self-esteem issues are often lucky if they manage to establish any friendships whatsoever. For many of these students, school would be far more manageable if they were simply allowed to participate academically, while not necessarily socially. Many students would actually benefit from being allowed to maintain their own identities, utilizing schools strictly as sources of knowledge, like libraries with instructors, while being permitted to seek social outlets outside of school, with others who share their values and interests.

READ MORE FROM HILLSBOROUGH, NORTH CAROLINA:

Schoolyard bullies and their victims: The picture fills out.

http://www.csmonitor.com/2004/0512/p01s03-ussc.htm

SOLUTION 27:

REDUCE SCHOOLS' PRACTICE OF ORGANIZING STUDENTS INTO ARTIFICIAL CATEGORIES, WHILE REQUIRING MORE INSTRUCTIONAL OPTIONS UTILIZING TEACHER FACILITAION AND STUDENT SUBJECT MASTERY.

28.

GIFTED = AVERAGE, AVERAGE = SLOW

Before the enactment of Public Law 94-142, the Education of all Handicapped Individuals Act of 1975, schools were free to prohibit access by students who happened to fall below certain intellectual cutoff score levels. Before the enactment of this law, it was primarily students identified as "gifted" who were often accorded special programming, attention, and services. However, following this legislation, suddenly less funding was appropriated for these students, with far more being earmarked for "special" education of students with learning deficits. Those with learning *strengths* were now presumed to require less "special" assistance. Concurrent with this change is the fact that, for the past 25 years, America's children have been able to access greater and greater amounts of information with little or no effort. Today, televisions often remain on for most of the time the occupants are at home, with factual information being imparted by both newsworthy and entertainment programs continually. Computer usage has also exploded from occasional usage at the local library to multiple times per day in ones own home, often for hours at a time. Even if these and other information sources are not being utilized for high-level academic research, they are, nevertheless, serving to fill children's heads with far greater amounts of information than was ever accessible to those from any previous generation.

Academic instruction, further, has come to include far more complex concepts at the elementary level than most American adults learned before late high school or college. There is no reason to believe, however, that the majority of America's kids are unable to absorb all of the information being made available to them. In the midst of all of the low test scores and other negative projections of today's students' capacity to learn, the real truth is that today's students are actually *smarter*. Due to this inescapable condition of knowledge "saturation" in today's society, there are actually many more students who would qualify as "gifted," based on their level of knowledge, than ever before. This would include students who demonstrate above average intelligence in one or more cognitive areas. However, due to reordered priorities coupled with rigid grade level parameters, these brilliant students make up most American classrooms today, with the smart kids being considered merely "average" by most of their teachers. By America's schools failing to accord many advancement opportunities to these students, the students with average abilities are too often deemed "slow." One of the biggest difficulties related to American school funding and performance concerns the ever-growing number of students who are identified for special education services, most as "learning disabled."

In reality, the odds of the occurrence of these handicaps in normal learning increasing from approximately 7% nationally, to figures nearing 20%, is actually mathematically unfeasible. Nevertheless, due to America's schools over-identification of average learners as "disabled" based on subjective criteria has created a generation of "victims." Further, teachers have grown so accustomed to perceiving their above-average and gifted kids as average, many have been rendered incapable teaching their students who require more than "once over" instruction. A big part of why this travesty is allowed to occur is the lack of sufficient federal and state oversight of American schools' delivery of special education.

    Too often, however, America's schools exploit this federally-defined category, with its corresponding mandated special education services, to include *all* students who "fail to perform at grade level," even when this failure is due to the students' "grade-level" teachers instructing at "above grade-level" expectations, or other reasons. As a result, a growing number of students with average intelligence and learning ability are being routinely assigned this label dooming them to "below-level" instruction, usually for the remainder of their education. Meanwhile, most of America's students with superior promise are made to endure instruction that is often rigid, repetitive, and tedious.

READ MORE FROM PORTLAND, OREGON:

Gifted students and the inclusive classroom

http://www.nwrel.org/msec/just_good/9/ch3.html

SOLUTION 28:

STOP REQUIRING STUDENTS WHO HAVE DEMONSTRATED ABOVE-AVERAGE ABILITY IN A GIVEN SUBJECT TO ENDURE AN ENTIRE SCHOOL YEAR OF UNNECESSARY INSTRUCTION, THEREBY ALLOWING TEACHERS TO CONCENTRATE THEIR SKILLS ON ACTUALLY TEACHING THOSE STUDENTS WHO TRULY NEED THEM.

29.

DE-EMPHASIS ON STANDARDIZED TESTS

In June 2004, the Chicago Public Schools failed to permit the 8th grade graduation of a number of their students who had failed to demonstrate minimum performance levels on the Iowa Test of Basic Skills, a standardized measurement of student achievement utilized by this district to assess annual student performance. Ironically, *all* of these students had been awarded passing grades in the same subjects they were identified as having *"failed"* on the ITBS. The parents were outraged and protested the district's action. Many were interviewed on the evening news where none mentioned the apparent lack of *instruction* to their children, only that their kids were being prevented the *experience* of participating with their grade-level peers. This instance, however, is just one of countless glaring examples of the huge disparity in America's schools' actual performance compared to their level of performance accountability to American society.

For reasons that defy logic, America's schools have adopted minimum performance standards of student achievement, yet still permit their *teachers* to adhere to differing standards, in fact *their own* standards, in assessing their students' academic progress toward these goals, despite the potential significance to the students' lives. There has long been much resistance, generated by teachers, to "teaching to the test," as though this would somehow result in cheating or substandard instruction. Still, there is probably no other institution in the world whose workers actively seek to resist working toward the organization's defined industry standards.

America's Schools, being pressured by teachers' unions, continue to permit instruction, grading, student promotion that is based solely on the whim of its teachers, regardless of how inconsistent with District or state instructional objectives. Even the current "No Child Left Behind" legislation mandates that threatens to impose severe penalties on schools failing to demonstrate annual "Adequate Yearly Progress" of their students, has done little to address this phenomenon.

While the week before graduation was no time to suddenly crush the hopes and dreams of the parents planning their children's graduation parties, the ongoing deception of these parents throughout their children's educational careers is unforgivable. Currently, most standardized measures of academic achievement prescribe specific performance levels in Reading Comprehension, English Language Usage, Mathematical Computation, and Science Reasoning, with some additionally requiring Social Science knowledge. Virtually none require assessment of student achievement in Art, Music, Computers, Drama, Health, or Physical Education, subjects that typically take equal precedence, while also occupying equal time, in many schools. It defies logic that state's "learning goals" are inconsistent with the same state's prescribed measurements of student learning. If these two standards were better coordinated then the practice of "teaching to the test" would simply become the "industry standard."

READ MORE FROM THE WASHINGTON POST:

Let's Teach to the Test

http://www.washingtonpost.com/wp-dyn/content/article/2006/02/19/AR2006021900976.html

AND

READ MORE FROM THE GEORGE LUCAS EDUCATIONAL FOUNDATION:

What Are Some Types of Assessment?

"What is evidence-based assessment? Is it standardized tests? Is it portfolios? If portfolios are a part of evidence-based assessment, what else is necessary? Reflections? Work samples? Best work?"

http://www.edutopia.org/modules/Assessment/types.php

SOLUTION 29:

MAKE REQUIRED STANDARDIZED TESTS AN INTEGRAL PART OF SCHOOLS' INSTRUCTION AS THE FINAL EXAMS, INSTEAD OF AS EXTRANEOUS UNNECESSARY IMPOSITIONS ON SCHOOLS' "REGULAR" INSTRUCTION.

30.

ATHLETICS:
THE SELLING OF A SCHOOL'S SOUL

Unfortunately, along with America's schools' failing to devote their efforts primarily on *required* areas of instruction, most high schools have made an even greater departure, by literally "selling out" to the standards of another organization, one with no academic origins. I refer to the NCAA, the National Collegiate Athletic Association. This is the organization dictates all of the rules for the athletic participation both of America's students and their schools. It's no secret that, to America's high schools in particular, athletics is big business, and so lucrative for most schools to consider sacrificing. More than any other school function, it's their athletic teams that generate the largest proportion of extra (and often unaccounted for) revenue, including entry fees, concessions, merchandise, and more. Many school leaders rely heavily on the "slush fund" resulting from these events to cover everything from building incidentals to major operating costs. Perhaps this explains why athletes and their coaches are frequently held in such high esteem by school administrators and board members. The NCAA not only controls schools' athletic participation, but also dictates which students will qualify for college athletic scholarships. In doing so, they further prescribe specific high school course completion requirements and minimum letter grades for students to be eligible for these awards.

Unfortunately, in far too many economically-challenged American communities, parents and educators place all of their hopes and dreams for their students on their ability to succeed athletically, as their best potential avenue out of poverty. In doing so, however, they are too often seduced into permitting significant compromise and subversive falsification of students' documented performance in their zeal to "help a kid out." In order to meet NCAA high school graduation and scholarship guidelines, Chicago Public Schools and countless other school systems now requires that *all* of their high school students complete Algebra, Geometry, Advanced Algebra/Trigonometry, two years of the same foreign language, Physics and Organic Chemistry, as a condition of graduation, *regardless* of cognitive ability. Instead of retaining students with lesser abilities until they are able to master all of these prescribed courses, the students are, instead, placed into "dummy" courses, such as "Basic Math" or "Basic Science," while their transcripts still reflect the NCAA course titles. This is fraud, and is misleading to the students, the parents, and the NCAA alike. Apparently, no one is counting on these students being able to make it into college on their own academic merits, while no one is tracking how many of these high school "graduates" are subsequently unable to pass basic college entrance exams written at the "GED" level.

  This practice of compromising course content, meant intended to not hold back "gifted" athletes with substandard academic skills, occurs with a "wink and a nod" daily between college recruiters and high school and coaches and others. Sadly, one can only imagine the dismay by an untold number of these students, who subsequently fail to attain star status on the playing field, only to discover that their high school transcripts document courses they have never taken and could never pass. If one of these student athletes also has a documented learning disability requiring special education, the student is typically denied adequate educational services available until the age of 21, in order to meet these rather unrealistic NCAA standards.

READ MORE FROM TYLER, TEXAS:

SCHOOLS' ROLE IN FUNDING CRISIS

http://www.tylerpaper.com/site/news.cfm?newsid=16473405&BRD=1994&PAG=461&dept_id=226369&rfi=6

SOLUTION 30:

KEEP THE NCAA OUT OF THE BUSINESS OF EDUCATION, WHILE HOLDING SCHOOLS ACCOUNTABLE FOR ANY AND ALL FALSE CREDITS AWARDED TO STUDENTS FOR CLASSES THEY DIDN'T PASS IN THE PURSUIT OF ATHLETIC GREATNESS.

31.

"TRYOUTS" = DENYING STUDENTS THEIR RIGHTS

America's schools, and all that they offer, are intended for *all* students within their boundaries. They are in no way meant to be exclusive "clubs," for which those who pay certain membership fees are entitled to greater participation than those who do not. Nevertheless, year after year, certain students are accorded preferential and selective treatment for which *all* taxpayers are forced to go along. One glaring example is the issue of student "tryouts" and "cuts" permitted for athletic teams, and other school activities, a practice that is both unfair and unwarranted. In the case of athletics, this is also another outgrowth of NCAA rewards to schools producing high performing athletic teams and "stars."

Coupled with this factor, significant public recognition is also accorded to coaches who manage to bring their schools' sports teams to championship status, regardless of cost. Unfortunately, these accolades are frequently unjustified and disingenuous. After all, what coach should not expect to exceed when being permitted to hand-pick all of the participants? This is no great feat. What would, instead, be worth celebrating is coaches who manage to achieve superior performance with teams that utilize *all* of the students in their schools who seek to play. In many high schools, the football coaches focus the majority of their efforts on cultivating a small handful of players, while relegating the remainder primarily to "benchwarmer" roles, if they are allow them to play at all. This type of "selective encouragement" also occurs with basketball teams, cheerleading squads, and countless other competitive school groups, as well.

This is both emotionally damaging to students while also fiscally unfair to the parents and other taxpayers. No student in a public school in America should be accorded preferential treatment, nor denied the opportunity to participate fully in *any* school organization if they so desire. There are countless private sports and artistic performance establishments where private paying students can be given this level of special recognition. There are also likely some public school coaches who should consider relocating their careers to these entities to one of these organizations, particularly if their primary goal is personal glory. Meanwhile, America's public school system is no place for only a very few chosen students to be given the chance to shine, at the expense of all the rest.

READ MORE FROM MADISON, WISCONSIN:

More on the Elimination of No-Cut Freshman Sports

http://www.schoolinfosystem.org/archives/2005/08/index.php

SOLUTION 31:

DISCONTINUE DENYING ANY STUDENT THE RIGHT TO PARTICIPATE IN ANY SCHOOL ACTIVITY OR SPORT, WHILE ALSO REQUIRING ALL COACHES TO "PLAY THE HAND THEY ARE DEALT."

32.

BEHAVIOR EXPECTATION: *"GIRLS"*

Despite much research in the last few decades addressing "behavior management," including positive reinforcement, child-centered learning, team-building, and more, little has actually changed in terms of teacher expectations of student behavior. This is evidenced by the ever-increasing growing numbers of students being recommended, often by their schools, for Ritalin® or other anti-impulsivity medications, primarily due to a perceived inability to comply with classroom behavior expectations. Could this many children *really* need medical intervention to control their normal behavioral urges? If so, how ever did American's ancestors manage to survive the world up to this point? Suddenly, a huge percentage of American children, particularly its males, are being found to be in need of psychiatric intervention in order to succeed in school. Further, the disproportionate percentage of males identified for special education services, particularly African-American males, is staggering.

Part of the reason for this phenomenon is a teaching expectation in most schools that is based on a vision of everyone seated at desks in classes made up of 25 to 30 students, all *paying attention* at all times. In this highly idealistic teaching model there is little room for error, and little opportunity for making up for lost time caused by interruptions of any kind.

Unfortunately, in order for most teachers in America to be able to do their jobs of merely *presenting* all of the required instruction to all of their students in the time allotted requires that they have few, if any, distractions. Due to the amount of material teachers are required to cram into short increments of time each day to large groups of students, there is precious little time for special consideration for any student who fails to behave like the most typical, quiet and mannerly *little girl*. Many children, particularly male children and adolescents, are naturally more animated and vocal, with fewer inhibitions than many girls. Unfortunately for them, while these traits may be the very ones that led their ancestors to venture out to a new world, build a business, or survive numerous setbacks, these same inherited traits are now being treated as detriments in their descendents, requiring pharmaceutical intervention. America's schools have become so complex and demanding of both students and teachers that any child whose personality represents a departure from norm now risks being labeled, medicated, or removed to an alternative setting.

  Another factor contributing to this state of affairs is the expanded role America's schools are now expected to fulfill in society. Back when students with moderate to severe psychological conditions were simply excluded from most schools, they would often become the responsibility of their state departments of mental health. Somewhere around the time America's schools were first required to admit all students, regardless of handicapping conditions, the field mental health became considerably less responsible for the care of a significant number of America's mentally ill. Many handicapped adults suddenly became a part of the growing number of "street people," the homeless, as well as others, not truly capable of caring for themselves. Mentally ill individuals of school age, however, became largely the responsibility of America's public schools, even if their primary handicapping condition required medical, and not educational, intervention. As a result, a large number of students with severe mental disabilities today occupy both regular and special education classrooms throughout America's schools. In many cases these individuals' behaviors are beyond that which should be managed solely by individuals having no mental health and/or medical training. The behaviors exhibited by mentally ill students now being instructed along with other students are frequently highly irrational, unpredictable, and dangerous. Further, students exhibiting only mild behavioral idiosyncrasies derived from less severe psychiatric conditions are often placed into classrooms with student with more severe disorders, leading to their acquisition of additional and compounded behaviors and other problems.

One way America could rectify this dilemma would be for many of its schools' their current medical and psychological services to be reassigned to their state departments of health where they rightly belong. America's schools have a responsibility to ensure that they are, first and foremost, performing satisfactorily in their *primary* role of imparting instruction in each of the core academic subjects. Expenditures and resources for medical services are better provided by professionals who are governed by the AMA.

By ensuring that some of the more severe behavioral challenges are properly supported by *medical* personnel employed by *medical* facilities, school personnel could focus on providing education, instead of mental health services. Proper servicing of these students would, in turn, lead to greater a climate of greater freedom to explore, learn, and grow with less stringent behavioral restrictions, for those capable of these expectations.

READ MORE FROM ATLANTA, GEORGIA:

**No Running, No Jumping:
The War Against Boys in Our Schools**

http://www.worthynews.com/breakpoint/no-jumping.html

SOLUTION 32:

*SCHOOLS MUST DISCONTINUE ACCEPTING THE ROLE OF MEDICAL PROVIDER AND RECOGNIZE THAT INSTRUCTIONAL GAINS CANNOT BE MET UNTIL MEDICAL ISSUES HAVE FIRST BEEN RESOLVED.
ALLOW STUDENTS MORE FREEDOM TO SPEAK, MOVE, AND EXPRESS THEMSELVES WHILE MAKING LEARNING MORE INTERACTIVE.*

33.

UNEQUAL INSTRUCTION AND OTHER SCHOOL SERVICES

With all Americans being entitled to equal access to all governmental services, it only stands to reason that this would apply to its public school services, as well. There is a certain standard Americans have come to expect, for our highways, our roads, our fire and police protection, and our postal services. American citizens would tolerate nothing less than for these services to be equally available and *adequate* for all. In areas requiring more police protection, for example, Americans expect a larger police force; in areas with more highways, more road services; more communities experiencing more medical incidents, more emergency personnel, and so on. Unfortunately, when it comes to public schools, one's zip code, rather than need, has the greatest bearing on the amount and type of education available to one's children.

Despite a Constitution ensuring equality for all Americans, there remains a huge disparity in the quality of education in America's schools from one school to the next, often even within the same community. How many Americans realize, for example, that the number of high school course credits required for graduation varies from 18 to 24, even within some states? Or, that while in some high schools students enjoy courses in Graphic Design, Latin, Biochemistry, and Classical Orchestra, those in other high schools, often only a mile or two away, may not? Frequently, these disparities follow not only socioeconomic lines, but racial lines, as well. Too often students attending one of America's "disadvantaged" schools have already realized fewer opportunities to experience the world than many of their same-aged peers, yet are then further penalized by not being afforded as many learning opportunities from their schools as other students of the same age, attending public school in the same state. In the case of special education, student placement options in poorer schools are often limited well beyond that which is actually allowed by federal law, such as the provision of a number of learning accommodations such as occupational therapy, individual student aides, extended school year services, technological devices, and more. Students with the same or similar disability diagnoses residing in differing school boundaries very likely receive very disparate levels of educational support for the same conditions, leading to very different degrees of educational progress. Unfortunately, these exceptionally needy students are permitted no opportunity to transfer to a school better able to meet their needs services without paying "out of district" tuition. In a nation that insists on the daily recitation of the words, *"liberty and justice for all,"* in all of its schools, how ironic that this system maintains a practice of inequality that is neither fair nor justified.

READ MORE FROM SAN DIEGO, CALIFORNIA:
Leave No School Behind
"Much has been written about funding inequities in America's public schools. Although California's courts have required that the state equalize spending among school districts, many inequalities remain. Some of the most troubling occur within districts. " http://www.acorn.org/index.php?id=367

SOLUTION 33:

OFFER ALL INSTRUCTION DEEMED NECESSARY AND APPROPRIATE FOR ALL STUDENTS AT ALL PUBLIC SCHOOLS IN AMERICA. RELEGATE ANY ADDITIONAL COURSES TO AN AFTER-SCHOOL ACTIVITY NOT INCORPORATED INTO SCHOOLS' REGULAR CURRICULUM.

34.

NO ADVANCED PLACEMENT ART CLASSES

At the same time America' schools are attempting to do too little for too many, they are also continuing to do more than necessary for those who do not actually need it. Consider that 15 to 20% of students whose academic abilities range from "above average" to "gifted." These students have demonstrated academic knowledge on standardized tests well above their same-aged peers. This would suggest that they are already in possession of much of the educational knowledge required of their grade level. Nevertheless, America's schools are typically highly resistant to promoting a student to the next grade level in lieu of requiring them to endure an entire school year of material; material that they have previously demonstrated that they *already know!* Schools, further, cling to the ideal that all students born within a 12-month period are at precisely the same developmental learning levels in *all* subject areas simultaneously, downgrading any student who fails to achieve at the highest end of this curve, while, at the same time, failing to consider the numerous brighter students who likely are bored out of their minds!

Students from the high end of the socioeconomic spectrum typically score the highest on standardized tests of academic achievement, making them a source of much pride by school district and state departments of education alike. In truth, most of these students have been raised in environments that causing them to be so knowledgeable and informed that their scores would likely be as high whether they ever attended school, or not. Too often, state education budgets are highly insufficient to meet the needs of *all* of its students, yet school leaders will often insist on preventing the higher-achieving students from moving ahead as they are able, rather than being "re-taught" material that they already know. This practice, which saps America's school resources unnecessarily, is carried out in the name of fairness, and to avoid having to plan of how to educate students whose age and academic grade-levels do not mesh perfectly. America's schools' version of fair education means everyone (within the same age/grade level) getting the same thing, rather than everyone getting what they actually *need.*

READ MORE FROM GOSHEN COLLEGE, INDIANA:

IS ART LEARNED FROM RULES?

http://www.goshen.edu/~marvinpb/arted/tc.html

SOLUTION 34:

REQUIRE THAT SCHOOLS GIVE STUDENTS THE ACADEMIC CREDIT THEY DESERVE FOR KNOWLEDGE THEY ALREADY POSSESS, AND STOP TAKING CREDIT FOR STUDENT ACHIEVEMENTS THAT ARE NOT OF THEIR DOING.

35.

GRADE "LEVELS" OFTEN UNBALANCED

One of the many obstacles to school improvement is our schools' steadfast reliance on methods that have consistently failed to work. Schools will never improve sufficiently until its leaders are willing to think outside of the proverbial box. Case in point: Ideally, in America, all will students learn to read by the end of first grade, to add, subtract, and write in complete sentences by the end of third. Unfortunately, this is too often simply not the case. Due to a number of factors, some student-related, some school-related, not all students designated as having "completed" one of the first three primary grades, (1st, 2nd, and 3rd), have actually managed to master these or a number of other grade-level requirements. However, due to public pressure, spurred by current research indicating that "retaining" students can have detrimental long-term effects, the students are almost always automatically bumped up to the next grade, regardless of what percentage of the curriculum was actually learned. However, these same stakeholders who endorse indiscriminate promotion of all students also likely presume that those who fail to learn all of their prescribed lessons are then given subsequent opportunities to do so. Unfortunately, choosing promotion over retention usually means leaving behind unlearned instruction, often to never encounter it again.

Perhaps most believe that all that is lost by skipping kids ahead is that some will have failed to demonstrate successful memorization of obscure names, dates, or difficult spelling words. This is because most are only considering one kind of learning. In reality, there are actually at least *two* basic types: Knowledge Acquisition *and* Skill Development. Unfortunately, even most state learning goals fail to recognize this distinction, resulting in a serious lack of consideration of students' instructional needs. What is most important to realize is that students must first acquire the *skills* of reading decoding, knowledge comprehension, word retrieval, verbal and written expression, and sentence structure, *before* being able to move forward in *any* subject area requiring communication in English. As well, students must be able to master the *skills* of addition and subtraction before they can be expected to understand multiplication or division, which, in turn, must be learned before moving forward with algebra.

Nevertheless, while this makes perfectly logical sense, it is almost never a consideration in developing school curricula. Instead, teachers are held to their state's strict instructional standards of their particular "grade levels," leaving little room for students who may simply need a little more individualized instruction to catch up to their peers. As a result, these students usually continue to fall farther and farther behind, so that by the time they reach the third or fourth grades they are either retained, or else identified as "learning disabled," often two equally poor choices for these kids. In schools that seek to limit their identification of students for special education services due to inadequate staffing and extra costs, these students will often be retained in the third grade, and sometimes again in the fourth grade. This eventually results in 15-year old sixth graders who have "aged out" of the elementary grades and so are hurriedly identified as "learning disabled" and then, appallingly, *"leapfrogged"* over the missed grade levels entirely and deposited into unsuspecting high schools. Once there, most will, of course, fail miserably, many dropping out before their junior year.

In other schools with greater resources, students are often more immediately identified as "learning disabled" while still in the third grade. In either case, more often than not, once a student is placed into "special education" for having fallen behind, they will almost certainly never catch up. Although federal law mandates that these students be provided instruction compatible with their same-*aged* peers, this is one law that continues to be severely compromised. That is because what is even more deeply ingrained in schools is the unwavering concept of *"grade levels."* Schools are so committed to maintaining the status quo that any student who does not happen to master a prescribed set of knowledge at the same time as the majority of students born during the same artificially-defined 12-month time frame are forced to pay dearly, often for the rest of their lives.

It is not merely that students must demonstrate performance compatible with that of other students born during the same year, meaning 6 months older or younger. Instead, depending on a student's birthday, they could be expected to perform compatible with students who are predominantly *10 or 11* months older or *10 or 11* months younger. In the case of a student's birthday placing them at the young end of this range, this often results in the student's academic performance being deemed substandard, while certain brighter students, particularly those born at the older end of this artificial "grade level" year, could be subjected to unnecessarily limited instruction, thereby compromising their long-range potential. A far more logical and fair process would be for students to be grouped by age *ranges* for each subject, although not necessarily the same groups for each subject area.

On the flip side, high schools throughout the nation are struggling to meet their financial obligations. Yet, most continue to cleave to a very costly and unnecessary practice intended more to fulfill the schools' role of "social club" than learning institution.

While there continue to be growing numbers of students each year who fail to attain minimum learning standards, there are also significant numbers who do. Nevertheless, instead of most high schools acknowledging their students who have demonstrated academic achievement beyond the high school level, thereby granting them proficiency credit and early graduation, they, instead, continue to direct their best resources and teachers toward "educating" these kids in material already mastered. Instead of freeing these students to go off to at least college, most having far more resources and sagging enrollments, they continue to lock these students unnecessarily into "grade levels" and "graduation requirements" designed more for the convenience of the teachers than the students or the taxpayers. In most cases, the majority of the instruction that a school's "honor students" are forced to "learn" during their junior and senior years are courses they will also be required to repeat during their first year or two of college, anyhow. Why are America's schools wasting precious school resources on kids who don't need them, instead of focusing on improving the performance of those who do? If they did then schools and state education departments couldn't brag about their high achievers, while allowing these students to remain longer than necessary soaking up curricular and extra-curricular resources intended for those who *really* need them.

While schools around the nation are on the verge of "resource bankruptcy" given the ever growing number of schools appearing on the No Child Left

Behind "watch list," they need to abandon their desire to "keep up with the Joneses" and start focusing on their real purpose for existing in the first place. Sadly, in America's schools' effort toward political correctness, they have all but done away with ability grouping, in lieu of "age grouping," even though this is the *very concept* on which classroom instruction and grade levels were developed in the first place. Back when schools were more likely to retain any student who failed to make the grade, "grade levels" remained fairly homogeneous in terms of ability levels. Now instead, today's schools' first priority is limited to uniformity of curricula, teacher contracts, and bell schedules, while students' individual learning needs have become secondary. How sad that so many of America's are now completely missing the point.

**READ MORE FROM
THE MANHATTAN INSTITUTE:**

Report: Holding Back Students Helps

http://daily.nysun.com/Repository/getmailfiles.asp?Style=OliveXLib:ArticleToMail&Type=text/html&Path=NYS/2004/12/08&ID=Ar00201

SOLUTION 35:

ALLOW NO STUDENT TO ADVANCE IN ANY SUBJECT UNTIL THEY DEMONSTRATE SUFFICIENT MASTERY OF THE PREVIOUS INSTRUCTION, WHILE ALSO NOT PREVENTING ANY STUDENT FROM ADVANCING THEIR KNOWLEDGE IN A SUBJECT ALREADY MASTERED SIMPLY BECAUSE OF THEIR BIRTHDAY.

36.

HIGH SCHOOL GRADUATES WHO CAN'T PASS COLLEGE ENTRANCE EXAMS

At the very least, Americans expect that their high schools are providing instruction compatible with college entrance. Most Americans would believe that any high school graduate, who completed all high school course requirements with at least a "B" average, had been educated sufficiently to be able to pass basic entrance tests at most state colleges and universities. Yet, unbelievably, this is quite often not the case. Although this has come to be a somewhat accepted, and even *expected,* phenomenon with certain exceptional athletes, it is not the standard Americans expect for its high school graduates, in general. Yet, in literally millions of cases, although students' high school transcripts may indicate that they successfully passed four years of English, a year each of Algebra, Geometry, Advanced Algebra, World History, U.S. History, Biology, Physics and Chemistry, these course titles and grades are less than genuine. In order to ensure that the majority of their students with substandard skills "complete" high school in four years, a large percentage of their instruction is actually so remedial and "off-level" from that reported on their transcripts, that, once graduating, many are unable to pass college entrance exams of the *same material.* This is nothing short of fraud that costs parents and the general public alike.

In order to enter any American college or university, every entering student must demonstrate a proficiency in English, Basic Math, and Writing by passing what is nothing more than a G.E.D. (General Educational Development) exam. The huge financial fraud being perpetuated by America's schools is based on the fact that the *parents* believe their children have actually mastered the given subjects. However, if they had truly *passed* Algebra, for example, they would then be able to pass Basic Math. Instead, adding insult to injury, when they fail to do so, they are then required by the colleges to take (and *pay for*) remedial courses that they must pass before being permitted to enroll in courses that will count toward a degree. The students might just as well not have wasted their time filling seats in their disingenuous high school classes, if they were going to be required to repeat the instruction again in college. More importantly, America's students, their parents, or the American taxpayers, are paying for replacement instruction that American high schools *falsely* documented that their students already received and passed. In any other industry in America this would be recognized for what it is: Grand larceny and consumer fraud.

READ MORE FROM ARIZONA:

Exit exam plight in Arizona Schools

http://www.kimberlyswygert.com/archives/001631.html

SOLUTION 36:

MAINTAIN A CONSISTENT AND DEFINED STANDARD OF COURSE INTEGRITY FOR ALL SUBJECT AREAS.

37.

NO GRADE-TO-GRADE COLLABORATION

As if the "course-completion" fraud depicted in the last chapter weren't enough, the amount of *duplication* of instruction and lack of continuity between grade levels that occurs in most American schools is like that which would be tolerated in no other business setting. In elementary school, as students pass from one grade-level to the next, their teachers almost never provide any subsequent input while learning little about their students' progress throughout the remainder of their schooling. This complete and deliberate lack of accountability for one's professional efforts is incomparable to any other American business or service. For a task of so great and long-reaching importance as shaping the minds, and in turn, the lives, of our future adults, how could those accorded this task be permitted so little responsibility?

As students progress from elementary to middle to high school, even less coordination of instruction or teaching methods is perpetuated. The receiving teachers typically have no more knowledge of a student transferring from a school across the parking lot than one from across the country. What is even more disheartening, at a time when growing numbers of schools are suffering from financial ruin, is that America's high schools continue to provide instruction that is only going to be replicated during most students' first two years of college. Considering that most state education agencies oversee both their states' elementary and secondary education services and also their higher education services, this duplication of instruction seems both conscious and deliberate. Rather than permitting capable students to demonstrate their level of proficiency in a given subject, such as English, they are, instead, forced to re-take this, and a number of other courses for four years in a row, first in high school, and then again for 1 or 2 years in college.

As our costs of higher education continue to rise, why not allow students to bypass that which they have already learned?

**READ MORE FROM
LOUISIANA TECHNICAL UNIVERSITY:**

The Continuing Trouble with Collaboration: Teachers Talk

http://cie.asu.edu/volume6/number15/http://cie.asu.edu/volume6/number15/http://cie.asu.edu/volume6/number15/

SOLUTION 37:

ASSIGN EACH STUDENT AND INDIVIDUAL "CASE MANAGER;" A TEACHER WHO FOLLOWS AND IS HELD PARTLY RESPONSIBLE FOR THEIR ACADEMIC PROGRESS THROUGH THE GRADE LEVELS.

THE LEADERSHIP: MISGUIDED

"WHO DO THEY THINK THEY ARE?"

38.

SCHOOLS' AUTHORITY:

"IN LOCO PARENTIS,"

OR "DRIVING THE PARENTS CRAZY!"

On of the most unnerving, if not THE most insulting, aspects of our public schools is the legal premise of *in loco parentis*, a law that grants schools primary authority over students that actually *overrides* that of their parents during the school day, on school premises, and even while students are traveling to and from school. Most recently, this authority has been extended by the courts to *non*-school days, for *non*-school events, and on *non*-school premises, setting legal precedents that compromise even greater percentages of parents' already compromised legal freedoms.

One notable example of this is a recent highly publicized high school team hazing incident. In this case, an off-school activity, conducted by certain school athletes, albeit raucous, had been knowingly permitted to continue for several years with the full knowledge and unspoken consent of school district authorities. Nevertheless, with recent technology resulting in video cameras being as common as wristwatches, the entire incident was captured and shared with the world via the nightly news. Only then did the school's authorities decide to take any action. Despite their well-documented knowledge of previous serious injuries, police intervention and alcohol involvement the school had consistently taken the position of this event being "not our problem." After all, it occurred on a Sunday, at a forest preserve, and was not officially sanctioned.

Parents were also well aware of this long standing local rite of passage but believed it to be sanctioned by the school by virtue of the school's history of continuing to acknowledge the participants along with their *silent* approval of the event year after year. Resulting only from the national publicity, the school, for the first time ever, suspended the participants, and then brought more serious charges of expulsion and withdrawal of scholarships, while barring them from participating in the graduation ceremony. While these sanctions may seem rationale at first glance, in order to justify the school finally taking this action against their students' inappropriate conduct, two key factors related to this exercise of authority must first be examined more closely. One concerns the matter of the schools' sudden and inconsistent action toward the students; the other is toward the students' parents. The school's violation of both parties' civil rights is at stake in both cases. By declaring that their authority suddenly and without warning extended to non-school events on non-school grounds on non-school days, *superseding* that of the parents, the school denied the parents one of their most basic human rights, having already pillaged the much of the rest of their parenting time. Ironically, by claiming this authority, they placed themselves in a bit of a legal quandary. They publicly declared their legal liability, (a byproduct of authority), for events and premises over which they actually have no physical or supervisory control. Suddenly they were assuming responsibility for all of their students, 24-hours per day, 7 days per week, in virtually all settings, and for all events even remotely tied to the school, such as any party attended by multiple members of a school same team. *(Their liability insurance carrier probably wasn't consulted on this one!)*

In some of the most convoluted logic the school, and not the students' parents, were deemed to have the final authority over the kids' actions, while only the parents and students were held accountable. While the parents did go along with the event, it was only after being witness to years of the school's sanctioning it without reprimand or intervention of any kind. Imagine, as a parent, trying to uphold a higher authority than the school to one's teenagers. To have done so would have actually made the *parents* seem like the ones challenging the school's authority. Besides, the kids knew full well that the impending annual event was being touted openly at school, with the full knowledge of countless school employees. However, unlike the school staff, (none of whom had made any effort to alert either the police or the parents of any potential dangers, the parents never saw the entire student body together. Instead, most parents each were limited to seeing primarily their own teenager, for whom they granted permission for them to attend a Sunday afternoon long-standing school event. Being accustomed to worrying about their teenagers attending nighttime parties with unknown friends in strange homes, young drivers, drugs, and more, this was a battle most chose not to pursue. The students, as well, were merely following a precedent perpetuated by their school as being the officially-sanctioned rite of passage for them and all of their peers. How could any student seeking to fit in be expected to resist this pressure? The school failed miserably in their *in loco parentis* role any parent would expect of anyone with whom they delegated their children's care. They failed to inform the *real* parents of known dangers and severe potential consequences. Further, the school failed to adequately explain the extent of their authority, nor the absence of their intended responsibility for those in their charge.

**READ MORE FROM
LEXINGTON, MASSACHUSETTS:**

Parental Rights vs. Public Schools

http://www.liberator.net/articles/McElroyWendy/PRvPS.html

AND

READ MORE FROM "FOCUS ON THE FAMILY:"

Focus on the Family's Parental Rights Statement

http://www.family.org/cforum/fosi/education/pe/a0028958.cfm

***SOLUTION 38:**

REQUIRE THAT SCHOOLS CONCENTRATE ON ACADEMICS AND LET PARENTS DO THE PARENTING.

39.

TOO MUCH FUNDING SECRECY WITHIN SCHOOL DISTRICTS

One of the biggest cover-ups in America's schools has to do with how they spend their money. While school funding shortages continue to be touted as America's single biggest domestic crisis, how our America's schools spend the money they already have remains largely a mystery to the general public. The complex spending formulas for schools' usage of federal, state, and local funding is difficult to decipher. However, once funding amounts are delegated to the various departments within a school, there is keen pressure to maintain the same level of available monies from year to year. This means that whether or not the Art department actually *needs* new darkroom equipment, they would rather spend thousands of their school's operating budget unnecessarily than risk giving up these allocated funds to a needier department the following year.

While in the more sparsely funded school districts in America it is typical for students to have to share outdated textbooks and band instruments because there aren't enough to go around, school districts enjoying a higher tax base, often just a few miles away, students realize a continuous and lavish refurbishment of textbooks, instruments, uniforms, and equipment in every possible category. In addition to the generosity of their local taxpayers, many of these already well-financed districts benefit from numerous additional state and federal grants which should really have been awarded to schools more worthy. However, part of the reason the affluent schools are successful at procuring these monies is that most employ full time grant writers. Millions of additional dollars are awarded each year to America's less-needy schools, resulting in huge unnecessary expenditures. While many items are purchased with grant monies earmarked for such issues as *"fine arts appreciation,"* and *"creating safe schools,"* shouldn't these monies be awarded to the schools with having the truly greatest needs? Instead state departments of education appear to truly not consider need in awarding bonus funds for schools who can well afford to pay for them themselves.

In a recent news report, a Long Island, New York school administrator had found a way to abscond with over $1 million without it even being missed. In Illinois, the Governor Blagojevich's plea that his state's schools subscribe to a collective purchasing program that will save millions by buying supplies in bulk was quickly shot down by most school officials who were eager to not lose control of their "purchase order" power.

Read more from San Francisco,
(also Chicago, New York, Boston and Oakland):

The Agony of American Education:
How per student funding can
revolutionize public schools

http://www.reason.com/0604/fe.ls.the.shtml

SOLUTION 39:

REQUIRE THAT ANY SUPPLEMENTAL STATE SCHOOL FUNDS BE DISTRIBUTED BASED ON NEED, NOT SUBJECTIVE STATE-ADMINISTRATOR PREFERENCE.

40.

THE *"SQUEAKY WHEEL"* APPROACH TO "CUSTOMER"-SERVICE

Most American school districts have more highly-paid administrative authority figures than most local government municipalities. This is true even in the occasional "one-school" district. In Illinois, for example, several of its school districts pay 6-figure salaries to both a superintendent and a principal, while some also pay multiple assistant superintendents, assistant principals, and more. Nevertheless, despite this very top-heavy leadership structure, most school administrators actually have very little authority, and are almost completely beholden to others. All but the highest-ranking superintendent are beholden to this authority, while the superintendent is, in turn, beholden to the school board. The school board members, being the only elected members of this hierarchy, are each beholden each to only protecting their status by serving the needs of their most vocal and influential constituents.

Therefore, most school principals, department heads, directors of special education and other school district administrators are simply "middle managers" required to espouse all of the wishes of the superintendent, regardless of how these may conflict with their moral, legal, or ethical obligations to their unpopular decisions. These individuals are often expected to exercise their administrative designation to sign off on a number of policy matters for which they may not agree, in a deliberate effort to deflect responsibility for unpopular decisions. School board members are usually most concerned with maintaining the status quo by suppressing any noticeable controversy. One way this may be accomplished is by avoiding any conflicts compelling a teacher strike. Such an occurrence disrupts most communities in an incomparable way, compromising childcare and vacation schedules, costing citizen in real dollars in lost work time, cancelled airline tickets, and extended childcare costs, if any can be found. To avoid such a disruption, principals are warned not to make any extraordinary demands or even *requests* of teachers' time or duties. This means, for example, that if teachers do not wish to provide any special accommodations to students with disabilities in their classrooms, principals are hesitant to press the issue, regardless of any such dictates in state and federal laws. Most teacher contracts state that the teachers may remove any child from their classroom at any time, simply when they feel that the child is *"disrupting the learning environment."*

In most school districts in America, what carries far greater weight with school leaders than any education laws are their union contracts. These contracts are often agreed to by superintendents and school board members who have little understanding of how much of the wording of many of these contracts is actually in direct conflict with the schools' legal obligation to serve all of their students equally. Instead only those students whose parents have the fearlessness to make their complaints heard are ever granted the equitable treatment they deserve, such as reconsideration of a grade, a class placement, or a teacher assignment, usually only with a promise of secrecy to not share this "exception" with other parents.

READ MORE FROM NEW MEXICO:

An Interview with Joel Turtel, author of *Imposter* and *Public Schools, Public Menace.*

"The scariest thing about our public schools is that many of them are so good at deceiving parents into thinking they are giving our kids a decent education. If parents knew the real truth about public schools and the many ways these public schools can seriously harm their children, they would abandon the public schools in droves."

http://www.educationnews.org/writers/michael/An_Interview_with_Joel_Turtel_%20About_Public_Schools_Public_Public_Menace.htm

---

SOLUTION 40:

REQUIRE THAT WHENEVER A SCHOOL MAKES A CHANGE OR GRANTS A REQUEST ON A STUDENT'S BEHALF, THAT THE SAME CONSIDERATION IS ALSO ACCORDED TO ALL OTHER STUDENTS.

41.

PRINCIPALS ONLY KNOW ABOUT THEIR "REGULAR ED" STUDENTS

With the enactment of Public Law 94-142 in 1972, all students with disabilities became entitled to a Free Appropriate Public Education (FAPE), the same as their non-disabled peers. The Individuals with Disabilities Education Act in 1997 expanded this obligation to requiring that the students' home school be the first consideration for all school placement decisions. This means that the majority of America's schools now have a significant percentage of students with designated disabilities requiring special education services. Nevertheless, *no* additional training has been made a requirement of school principals or other administrators to ensure the appropriate delivery of these educational services to these students in their care. This is equally true of their training in other specialized areas, including services to non-native English speakers, as well.

College and university programs leading to School Administrator certification have actually changed very little in the past 40 years. No specific instruction or training in any of the specialized leadership and instructional needs of these students has been included. The one required School Law course required in most school administrator preparation programs rarely addresses the most predominant legal issue in America's schools, the inadequate delivery of instruction to student's with disabilities. This lack of required understanding has resulted in lengthy and costly litigation brought by parents of these students, believing that their school's administrators failed to adequately address their children's needs.

Too often, principals defer to district administrators to handle the supervision of all of the instruction and instructors of their students with disabilities, to the detriment of these students and their parents, and at the expense of the students' educational process.

READ MORE FROM NPR's Talk of the Nation:

Analysis: Special education in the age of national standards

http://www.susanohanian.org/show_special_commentaries.html?id=39

SOLUTION 41:

REQUIRE A COURSE IN THE MANAGEMENT AND OVERSIGHT OF THE EDUCATION OF STUDENTS WITH DISABILITIES, AND ALL OTHER SPECIAL POPULATIONS, BE INCLUDED IN ALL SCHOOL ADMINISTRATOR TRAINING PROGRAMS.

42.

THE SUPERINTENDENTS: "OUR WAY OR THE (VACATION?) HIGHWAY"

As if America's school superintendents do not have enough pressure from parents, teachers, principals, and school board members, they are also often dismissed in an almost ritualistic public fashion whenever they fail to effect desired change, when they make changes too quickly, or when problems that were in place long before they arrived are not quickly resolved. However, most school superintendents in America are employed under multi-year contracts, at guaranteed six-figure salaries for each year. When these professionals are then dismissed before the end of their tenure, usually when they disagree with the wishes or philosophy of their school boards, they then continue to be *paid* for the rest of their contracts, with taxpayer dollars, often even if they are dismissed with multiple years remaining!

There is even a standing joke in the world of school administrators about dismissed superintendents taking turns living out the remainder of their contracts in tropical locales, only to be rehired elsewhere at the end of their paid "vacations," and the cycle is repeated. While state and local governments are continually being blamed for schools' lack of resources, frivolous and misguided school boards are actually guilty of committing these expensive decisions on a regular and frequent basis, and with little accountability for the reduction of educational resources their decisions create.

READ MORE FROM PITTSBURGH, PENNSYLVANIA:

Schools need class in firing chiefs

http://www.pittsburghlive.com/x/pittsburghtrib/s_283400.html

SOLUTION 42:

ELIMINATE SCHOOL SUPERINTENDENTS' MULTI-YEAR EMPLOYMENT CONTRACTS, AT LEAST UNTIL THEY HAVE DEMONSTRATED A FEW YEARS OF CONSISTENT AND SUCCESSFUL LEADERSHIP WITH THE SAME SCHOOL DISTRICT

43.

STATE DEPARTMENTS OF (LITTLE) EDUCATION

As if school district governance weren't a big enough problem in terms of school mismanagement, what occurs at the state level of educational governance is most often much worse. There is a common perception, particularly by parents, that state education agencies (SEAs) exist to oversee school systems and ensure their compliance with State and Federal education laws; sort of an American Medical Association (AMA) of schools. Not so. Just as educators are not subject to any *Hippocratic Oath*, there is no ethical oversight of schools by any governmental body that is sufficiently comprehensive to ensure that the rights of America's students are being met by their schools.

Further, there is a condition of conflicting authority creating a level of cognitive dissonance borne out of *state* governance and oversight of primarily *federally*-compelled laws that are usually added to state rules, sometimes in congruence with, ands sometimes directly opposed to other state policies, with little or *no* direct federal oversight.

While there exists within these laws a *"due process"* procedure wherein parents may bring their complaints with their children's schools to their state education agencies, they must due so at their own expense, including funding their own legal counsel, while the school districts' attorneys, hired to defend schools from any wrongdoing, are paid for with *education tax dollars*. While few issues are resolved using this process to the parents' satisfaction, the overwhelming number of due process hearings, which are presided over by SEA officials, and mediated by current or former school district employees, are settled in favor of the schools, regardless of how many federal and state education laws the schools may have knowingly violated.

**READ MORE FROM the
National Council for Accreditation of Teacher Education (NCATE):**

"Accreditation is inadequate to address accountability."

http://www.ncate.org/boe/0413_chea.asp?ch=150

SOLUTION 43:

ESTABLISH LOCAL BRANCHES OF FEDERAL OFFICES OF EDUCATION TO BE RESPONSIBLE FOR UPHOLDING NATIONAL EDUCATION STANDARDS. ALLOW ALL SCHOOL DUE PROCESS COMPLAINTS TO BE BROUGHT BEFORE THE FEDERAL COURT AND NOT TO THE SAME GOVERNMENT AGENCY RESPONSIBLE FOR ANY POTENTIAL GRIEVANCES.

44.

AMERICA'S SCHOOLS HAVE TOO MANY "*COOKS*"

When it comes to actually teaching kids, there are far too many individuals involved in directing this process besides the *teacher*. Unlike physicians, who are generally regarded as the final authority over their patients' medical care, teachers are permitted no such consideration. Now, one may believe that this is because teachers are required to complete far less education than medical doctors to attain their roles. This is not entirely true. Simply completing a bachelor's degree in almost any other academic subject does not require so stringent a list of undergraduate courses, nor include the requirement to work full-time for an entire semester in their chosen field, *unpaid*. This requirement is one of the primary obstacles preventing many working adults from entering the teaching field. Further, once completing these degree requirements, prospective teachers must also submit to multiple state exams in order to finally obtain their teaching credentials. Then, once employed, teachers are required to complete ongoing coursework continuing for the remainder of their careers in order to remain certified to teach. Further, teachers are afforded no guarantee of continued employment until they have worked for four years for the same school system, making them completely beholden to the wishes of their school administrators until crossing this milestone, but then freed almost completely from their constraints once they do.

By contrast, physicians are able to begin working as *paid* interns almost from the beginning of their medical training, are required no specific continuing education once licensed, and are paid more while in training than most teachers make after multiple years of service. As classroom teachers, these professionals who have already made significant sacrifice and commitment to serve children are then given almost no credit for having any judgment or decision-making authority over their jobs. They must teach *only* subject-matter prescribed by "state learning goals," must use *only* the textbooks and curriculum provided by their school systems, and must adhere strictly to prescribed schedules, behavior management methods, and school board policies related to course content, instructional methods, and student grading. While teachers are most often those blamed for the failure of America's schools to meet state-defined learning benchmarks, perhaps, state departments of education (typically staffed by bureaucrats, not educators), should consider giving the professionals best trained in *teaching* more of the decisions affecting student learning.

Anyone who has ever tried to teach anything to a group of kids knows that some methods work for some kids, and some for others. Some kids grasp concepts quickly, while others need more repetition, descriptive examples, and a slower pace. By requiring one teaching schedule, one set of learning standards, and one set of grading criteria for all teachers, to be used with all of their students America is only stifling teachers' ability to do the jobs they have been hired to do.

**READ MORE FROM
THE BROOKINGS INSTITUTE:**

"Decisions made now about the content of reading and mathematics will have long term consequences, not only for students and schools, but for society as a whole."

http://www.brookings.edu/press/books/curriculum_debate.htm

SOLUTION 44:

ESTABLISH ONE CURRICULUM FOR EACH SUBJECT, BUT THEN ALLOW TEACHERS TO INSTRUCT IN THE WAY THAT THEY CHOOSE. RATHER THAN SCRUTINIZING TEACHER "LESSON PLANS" AND OTHER MEANS OF "PROVING" TEACHER EFFICACY, SCHOOL ADMINISTRATORS MUST ALLOW IMPROVEMENTS IN STUDENTS' STANDARDIZED TEST SCORES, FROM THE BEGINNING TO THE END OF THE SCHOOL YEAR. IN DOING SO, TEACHERS WILL LIKELY FIND WAYS TO ENSURE LEARNING BY ALL OF THEIR STUDENTS.

45.

TEACHER "EVALUATIONS:" THE ANNUAL "DOG & PONY SHOW"

When it comes to assessing teacher effectiveness, school administrators are actually quite restricted in how and when they may evaluate the performance of their teachers. The teachers' unions have managed to restrict these efforts to only two specified times per year, always with advance written warning, and then only for a very limited period of time. Nevertheless, most school administrators could still make far better use of these opportunities to determine the degree to which the teachers are meeting their students' needs. By analyzing the quality of teacher assignments, the students' demonstrated understanding, the quality of students' work completion, the students' rate of learning progress from last year, and the degree of teacher awareness of students' individual learning needs, administrators could gain far more insight into the actual instructional abilities of their teachers.

Instead, during these limited "classroom evaluations" most administrators focus almost completely on teachers' skills managing their students' behavior. While having some value, it does not begin to compare to teachers' abilities to impart needed instruction in a manner that is both understood and retained. Typically, teachers being "evaluated" will plan very predictable and simplistic lessons leaving little room for error or creativity. Students are often coached or even bribed in advanced to "perform" in a certain manner to assist the teacher with this brief "performance."

As a result, barring any major classroom disruption, and so long as the students appear interested in the instruction, the teacher can usually anticipate a satisfactory review, even though the administrator will likely never learn whether the students were able to subsequently use and apply the given instruction.

READ MORE FROM CLINTON, SOUTH CAROLINA:

Teacher pay tied to student progress?

http://www.cnn.com/2004/EDUCATION/01/14/teacher.salaries.ap/

SOLUTION 45:

BASE TEACHER PERFORMANCE ON STUDENT OUTCOMES, NOT ON PRE-PLANNED TEACHING "PERFORMANCES."

46.

RIGHT HAND, LEFT HAND, WHOSE HAND?

Due to the multiple "authorities" within most American school systems, a number of procedures, policies, and practices co-exist with cross-purposes. Each academic department answers to its own authority, often with each department existing in a vacuum, separate and apart from the other school departments and grade-levels. This results in the sharing of very little student information by educators who, nevertheless, work with the same students on a daily basis. While some school districts have sought to overcome this factor for certain student groups, it is still quite common in most American schools today, for a student's music teacher to have an extensive conversation with a parent regarding their child's hearing deficiency that *never* gets shared with any of his other teachers.

Further, a student's academic progress is almost *never* monitored from year to year, either by individual teachers, or by the school as a whole. Even standardized assessments prescribed by state education agencies fail to acknowledge the progress, or lack thereof, of any particular students. Instead, only "3rd grade Math scores," for example, are compared from year-to-year, but these scores are not from *the same students.* Meanwhile, standardized achievement progress by third graders in the same subject fourth grade, for example, is never considered. Once a teacher relinquishes students to the next grade level, they are rarely, if ever, asked to provide any input regarding the students' prior instruction, acquired knowledge, or preferred learning style.

Additionally, every level of school a system's hierarchy, from the school board, to district administrators, to building administrators, to teachers each develop and pursue their own set of goals and objectives, designed to meet various needs particular to their individual agendas, which often conflict or overlap with those of the other departments. Unlike the businesslike precision of most major corporations, school systems tend to create multiple and varying priorities to suit their various political, personal, and preferential needs.

For example, if a school board wants its schools to purchase particular instructional software, this decision might be made without any input as to the merits of this software from those who would be required to utilize it. If a superintendent should decide to discontinue providing certain costly special education programs, this might be done without any acknowledgement or understanding of how this modification might violates certain federal laws. If a teachers' union leader succeeds in including contractual wording that allows teachers to eliminate any child from their classes for any reason, then they, too, are risking such violations. Further, by school principals unknowingly authorizing their discipline deans to override federal limitations on accumulated days of school suspensions, or allowing their teachers to ban certain populations of students from fieldtrips, sports, or other school activities, they are authorizing crimes of which they likely have no knowledge or understanding.

Not that long ago, America's schools were one-room operations run almost exclusively by one teacher. Today, theoretically, in the interest of public service, America's schools have an elaborate system of school administrator networks, with most administrators earning in excess of $70,000 per year. The majority of superintendents earn well over $100,000, with many being paid in excess of most physicians, senators, or corporate executives, even though they defer most or all work to their underlings, while assuming as little responsibility for their schools' day-to-day operations as possible. This leaves them plenty of time for politics. Typically, the only time the American public ever hears of a superintendent is when a major crime is committed by students or staff requiring their public commentary.

Why does America need these high-priced politicians sapping resources meant for students' education? There are many who believe that America's schools would operate far more efficiently if more education dollars were directed toward the classrooms, via teacher salaries, materials, and facilities, than on school leaders who are too detached to truly impact the education of the students they are paid to serve.

READ MORE FROM THE NORTH CENTRAL REGIONAL EDUCATION LABORATORY (NCREL):

Viewpoints: School Leadership in the 21st Century: Why and How it is Important -

"Good Schools Need Good Leaders"

http://www.ncrel.org/policy/pubs/html/leadersh/goodschl.htm

SOLUTION 46:

RECORD EACH STUDENT'S ACADEMIC PROGRESS INTO A CENRTALIZED DATA BASE, WHILE ALL STAFF SERVING A PARTICULAR STUDENT PROVIDE ALL INFORMATION TO ONE CONSISTENT CASE MANAGER WHO MAINTAINS STUDENTS' INFORMATION AND PROGRESS THROUGHOUT THEIR EDUCATION.

THE TEACHERS (AND OTHER STAFF)

"WHAT GIVES THEM THE RIGHT?"

47.

LACK OF TEACHER TRAINING

Despite the excessive number of courses, exams, background checks, and countless other "hoops" teachers must go through to earn their positions, most receive little formal training that ensures their capacity to instruct actually students. State licensing exams assess only prospective teachers' knowledge of their subject matter and other basic academics, but no demonstration of an ability to actually teach anyone anything. What if obtaining a license to drive did not include assessing one's ability to actually drive a car?

Now, while a semester of "student teaching" is included with the teacher credentialing process, it is usually accomplished by having the teacher trainee co-teach in a classroom with another teacher, utilizing primarily lessons they had already developed. Even if the student teacher develops and delivers original lessons, this comes with no guarantee that the instruction was effective.

Most required college "teaching methods" classes consist largely of *"the blind leading the blind."* Since most American college professors of higher education have much firsthand experience with "lower education," many tend to rely on their students for most of their instructional topics by assigning each to develop and teach a lesson in their subject area to the classes of their college-aged peers. Unfortunately, teaching 3rd grade math to a group of captive college students has little bearing on ones' ability to teach the material to their intended subjects. Still, it is largely on this basis that most American teachers earn their teaching credentials.

Even in grading teacher trainees' "student teaching" performance, colleges give little consideration to how many students actually learned from the trainees' instruction, nor to what degree.

Physician-trainees learning to care for and preserve human growth and development, are not simply required to observe other doctors, while only occasionally trying a few procedures themselves. They are guided through years of collaborative training by more experienced professionals in a cooperative process. Unfortunately, America' schools and institutions of higher education do not share such a mutually cooperative relationship. Instead, America's colleges and universities merely provide future teachers an overview of the job utilizing instructors who have had little or no recent experience in the field themselves. The new teachers are then thrust out into the field without any measure of follow-up, to figure out for themselves a whole laundry list of issues of which they had never been taught, having to proceed toward their goal of tenure utilizing primarily a trial and error approach to meeting their students' learning needs.

> **READ MORE FROM UNIVERSITY OF WISCONSIN-OSHKOSH:**
> **Teacher training revitalized**
>
> http://www.weac.org/greatschools/2001-02/revitalized.htm

SOLUTION 47:

INCORPORATE REAL-WORLD TEACHER TRAINING INTO TEACHER CERTIFICATION REQUIREMENTS, INCLUDING A PAID "TRAINING YEAR," WITH NEW TEACHERS BEING GIVEN THE OPPORTUNITY TO DEMONSTRATE AN ABILITY TO ACTUALLY TEACH BEFORE BEING FULLY CREDENTIALED.

48.

LACK OF OWNERSHIP FOR STUDENT OUTCOMES

In order for any other business in America to succeed requires a strong sense of responsibility and accountability from all parties. Any other professional service is goal-oriented, with an emphasis on successful outcomes. Not so the profession of teaching, which places the responsibility for any success or failure almost exclusively on the *recipients* of the service. If a student "earns" an "F" this is almost never attributed to any failures on the part of the teacher, but only of the student. Recent "No Child Left Behind" legislation has attempted to address this issue by holding schools and teachers more directly responsible for student learning outcomes. Nevertheless, students who fail to learn to read or write continue to be "socially promoted," with their teachers simply deferring their own lack of instructional achievement onto those of the next grade level.

What is even more frustrating is a system that is responsible for America's very future permits this complete lack of accountability. First, students' letter grades are assigned based solely on the teachers' own prerogatives, and so are frequently based more on student "behaviors," such as work completion, attendance, and participation, than on any actual measurement of the students' acquisition of the prescribed knowledge. Moreover, the official measurement of a school's performance is their students' achievement on standardized tests. Nevertheless, these tests are not tied to student instruction or even to state learning goals, in most cases.

Much has been publicized about teacher bemoaning their being expected to "teach to the tests." However, if, as a nation, we have determined that our primary goal for our students is for them to be able to demonstrate sufficient knowledge of the material measured by these tests, then why do we allow our schools to permit teachers to resist making this instruction their first priority?

Further, why do we give equal attention to subjects not measured by these assessments, even for our students who have failed to master these first-priority learning goals? Why do we overload classrooms with students who have failed to master these primary benchmarks, rather than affording them more individualized instruction to help them achieve at the desired levels? Finally, why do we continue to support teachers and schools structures that fail to produce student results, while continuing to recognize that calling students "5th graders" who only read at the 1st grade level does not truly make them 5th graders?

**READ MORE FROM
THE U.S. DEPARTMENT OF EDUCATION:**

Promising practices: New ways to improve teacher quality -
Improving Teacher Accountability
and Incentives

http://www.ed.gov/pubs/PromPractice/title.html

SOLUTION 48:

TIE STUDENTS' GRADES TO ACTUAL STANDARDIZED TEST PERFORMANCE, MAKING TEACHING INSTANTLY MORE ACCOUNTABLE AND LETTER GRADES MORE EQUITIBLE, WHILE ALSO REMOVING MUCH OF THE SUBJECTIVITY FROM BOTH THE INSTRUCTION AND TEACHER PERFORMANCE EVALUATIONS.

49.

UNION RULES: *"THE UNION RULES!"*

When it comes to student welfare, those most directly responsible for student care, their classroom teachers, are protected by an organization that places a higher priority on protecting their own than on needs than on those whom their teachers are hired serve. Not that they promote any actual student endangerment, but teachers' unions do little to actually ensure appropriate student outcomes if doing so interferes with the interests of their members. Now, the two largest education organizations in America, the National Education Association (NEA) and the American Federation of Teachers (AFT), would argue that they care more about students than do most school leaders. They often assert that without union regulations America's schools would compel even greater class-sizes, demand more excessive teacher responsibilities, and provide even fewer classroom supports. Perhaps. But the fact remains that America's public schools are severely constrained by the parameters of their teacher contracts that place stringent limitations on teaching hours, working conditions, and job responsibilities, while also compelling mandatory annual salary increases regardless of performance. Further, once a teacher attains "tenure" status, recently increased in most states to four years, they are almost completely insulated from termination for all but criminal acts. There is virtually no tracking of individual teachers' student outcomes on State and local assessments of student performance that are tied to employment evaluations.

Further, unlike most workers in other American work settings who must commit to 40-hour work weeks, for 50 weeks per year, most American teachers' workdays consist of 6 1/2 hours of at-work time, of which often no more than 4 or 5 hours are spent actually instructing students. In departmentalized middle school and high schools this would equal five to six 50-minute class periods. In elementary schools this would account for the time students are dismissed to P.E., Music, and Art classes. In addition, teachers only work approximately 180 days per year, which, at 5 hours per day, is equal to only 900 work hours per year. When compared to the typical 50-week work year, at an average of 5 work days per week, while considering only 6 actual work hours out of an 8-hour day, this still amounts to at lest 1500 work hours per year, in excess of 50% more that teachers, usually with less frequent salary increases and far fewer employment guarantees.

Still, despite teachers' shortened work day, long holiday breaks, and extensive time off work during the summer months to allow for ample instructional planning time, teachers are still accorded at least one class period per day for "planning." They are also periodically absent to attend offsite training during school hours, which might be tolerable if the students appeared to be benefiting. Unfortunately, financially-strapped schools with students who are performing below average must still adhere equally to these union demands.

What is particularly disturbing is that when these demands are detrimental to student welfare, they are still required to be adhered to by school leaders or face costly litigation, risk teacher strikes, or both. Many teacher union contracts, for example, dictate that teachers may dismiss a student from their classrooms at any time and for any reason, whenever they feel that a student is "interfering with the learning environment." Also, despite prescribed State learning goals to the contrary, most teachers are protected from "any interference with or imposition upon their classroom instruction."

While this poses concerns for the education of all students, it has serious implications for students with disabilities, in particular. Still, regardless of school boards' legal obligation to uphold Federal education laws, they will circumvent them without hesitation if to do otherwise would mean upsetting their local teachers' union. Of greater fear than State or Federal sanctions, is community outcry and loss of their elected school board positions should their teachers elect to strike.

Imagine if physicians' working conditions took precedence over patient welfare.

READ MORE FROM THE CITY JOURNAL OF THE MANHATTAN INSTITUTE:

How teachers' unions handcuff schools

"No education reform can succeed until teachers' unions stop demanding work rules that subvert education's basic building block: the interaction between teacher and students."

http://www.cityjournal.org/html/7_2_how_teachers.html

SOLUTION 49:

REQUIRE THAT SCHOOL BOARDS IMMEDIATELY CEASE ACCEPTING ANY TEACHERS' UNION CONTRACTS CONTAINING WORDING THAT COMPROMISES SCHOOLS' LEGAL OBLIGATIONS TO THEIR STUDENTS.

50.

TEACHING WITH A *"TEAMSTER"* MENTALITY

Unfortunately, what accompanies most labor union organizations is the fairly rigid "teamster" mentality of its members. In many settings this would have no negative effects on work production or resulting work product. Inherent to the successful education of human lives, however, is the willingness of the instructors to show compassion for their students, to go the "extra mile," to do whatever it takes to ensure student success. This requirement is seriously compromised by an organizational system that limits student-teacher interactions to prescribed time frames, while placing teachers in the predicament of having to choose between their loyalty to their students and their colleagues. Unfortunately, as most of its teachers will attest, American schools are largely political entities. The only way for a new teacher to survive is to go along with the crowd, at least until attaining tenure. This means that trying to achieve greater student results, taking extra measures to meet students' needs, or going out of one's way by voluntarily working beyond union workday limitations, will only results in one's colleagues combining forces to compel the teachers' removal for failing to be a "team player."

Teacher time-restrictions are one of the greatest obstacles to school district improvements. Most proposed means of improving student outcomes require additional use of teachers' time. While many teachers would be willing to provide these additional services, they have been conditioned to consider doing so only for additional compensation. Further, any new administrative directives related to instruction, record keeping, or classroom management must first meet union approval or else accept an *"It's not my job"* response.

READ MORE FROM TEXAS A&M UNIVERSITY:

Fund and Games
Will the lege cheat on school finance?

http://grimpeur.tamu.edu/pipermail/csps/2003-December/000182.html

SOLUTION 50:

MAKE AVAILABLE ADEQUATE ADDITIONAL FUNDS FOR TEACHER OVERTIME PAY, WHILE ALSO PROVIDING INCENTIVES TO TEACHERS WHOSE STUDENTS' ATTAIN OPTIMAL SCORES OF ACADEMIC ACHIEVEMENT.

51.

AUTOMATIC RAISES –
WHETHER OR NOT ANYONE LEARNS

One final word about teachers' automatic salary increases: Granted, teacher shortages are rampant and there has to be some incentive to recruit and retain good teachers. But that's just it. There are plenty of *good* teachers who have left the field out of frustration, while plenty more remain who likely do not deserve the compensation level they have managed to attain. In no other industry are those who provide a product or service rewarded regardless of the outcomes of their efforts.

Currently, while more strident measures have been implemented recently that are meant to ensure greater school accountability for student outcomes, these measures still are only minimally tied to the performance of particular teachers. In most cases, student results are measured by subject-area or grade-level, only. Students' math scores, for example, are rarely tied to their most recent math instructors to determine any statistical differences between teacher outcomes. Teachers would argue that doing so would be highly unfair, since this would not take into account a whole host of factors outside of the teachers' control, such as students' academic histories, environmental and socioeconomic factors, as well as prior teaching failures. All things considered, however, it would seem quite relevant to know if one particular math teacher's students consistently scored higher on the Math portion of the S.A.T. than another's.

For example, instead, teacher performance is assessed largely on factors completely unrelated to their student learning outcomes. A typical performance evaluation, usually conducted only of non-tenured teachers, assesses primarily teacher's classroom (behavior) management, organization, classroom appearance, and lesson delivery. While these are all valid factors, a teacher's performance during only *one* lesson during on one day should not override all consideration of their resulting student outcomes, yet it does, almost without exception.

Rather than discouraging good teachers, a system that rewards merit instead of longevity would likely attract those most confident in their abilities to teach students and to effect measurable growth.

READ MORE FROM THE NEW YORK POST:

The teacher pay myth

http://www.manhattan-institute.org/html/_nypost_teacher_pay_myth.htm

---

SOLUTION 51:

BASE TEACHER SALARY INCREASES ON HOW WELL THEY TEACH, NOT MERELY HOW LONG THEY HAVE ONLY ATTEMPTED THE JOB.

52.

INSTRUCTION BASED ON TEACHER CONVENIENCE

There is an overriding assumption by parents and the general public alike that schools place the needs of students first and foremost above all else. It's the platitude that's repeated in school vision and mission statements throughout America. One thing this assumption promotes is the idea that if the kids would just behave and follow the rules that they would succeed, since, after all, schools are designed to ensure their success.

Not so. Not only is this not happening, it is not even being attempted. Somehow, in the translation from schools' original ideal *of "Send us your children and we'll make each of them whole,"* to the reality of managing several hundred children in one facility each day, "school" has become more about crowd control than about imparting knowledge. In order to live up to their assigned responsibility containing several hundred youth for seven hours each day, while also appeasing a few hundred union-invested employees, most decisions made by school leaders give very little consideration to the individual needs of their students or their parents.

The number and types of classes or subjects taught, class sizes, arrangement of the school day, selection of teaching materials, and student access to resources are all group decisions, with little or no individuation of instruction or services. This is just as true for special education students, whose instruction is federally mandated to be based on individualized educational goals. In reality, only the most severely disabled students actually receive anything resembling individuation of their education, contingent upon the degree of uniqueness of their disabling conditions. Despite federal and state disability education laws to the contrary, most schools in America still lump students together by similar ability or disability needs, while also frequently limiting disabled students' access to instructional opportunities based primarily on student behavior or for teacher convenience.

The number and scope of these departures from education law by the majority of America's schools is extensive. Special education classes are often denied access to their schools' science labs; students of certain disability categories are often denied participation in fieldtrips because of teacher fears of public embarrassment; much instruction to students with disabilities does not adhere to state learning goals and grade-levels because its easier to teach the more difficult students "off level."

At one time, parents expected their children's schools to do little more than expose their children to the fundamentals of reading, writing, and arithmetic. Until the mid-1960's America's schools could exercise their option of dismissing students who did not, or could not, meet minimum academic standards. Those who remained, therefore, were comprised of a more compliant and academically-promising group. However, America's schools today play a far greater role in shaping the lives and destinies of tomorrow's adult citizens. Gone are most of students' daily household chores that occupied the greater portion of many young people's lives. They have been replaced with higher academic expectations, a much broader definition of what is considered "minimal" instruction, including the somewhat unrealistic American expectation of a college education for all. No longer is any American public school legally permitted to exclude any student from any opportunity afforded to another, yet, the reality is that America's schools are notorious for doing so blatantly, daily, and without fear.

> **READ MORE FROM *USA TODAY*:**
>
> **CHEATING OUR KIDS: HOW POLITICS AND GREED RUIN EDUCATION**
>
> *"Bad schools are everyone's problem, author says"*
>
> http://www.usatoday.com/news/education/2005-11-29-cheating-our-kids_x.htm

---

SOLUTION 52:

PERMIT ALL STUDENTS TO PARTICIPATE IN ALL PROGRAMS AND SERVICES PROVIDED BY THEIR SCHOOLS.

53.

COED PE / LOCKER ROOM SUPERVISION AND SAME SEX ATTRACTION

As our awareness of individuals' sexual preferences grows ever more commonplace, no longer is there a stigma attached to being a gay teacher. Modern psychiatry has confirmed no greater preponderance in homosexuals than heterosexuals for molesting children. Therefore, there is no reason to worry that there are now far more homosexual teachers than ever before, right?

Not so fast. There is one aspect of school instruction, which, if not addressed, will continue to serve as an outlet for unwelcome sexual contact. Consider, if you will, the gross inappropriateness of heterosexual male P.E. teacher having his office situated in the girls' locker rooms overlooking the girls' changing area. While this would never occur, at the same time, adult *females*, many who happen to be homosexual, (and therefore attracted to females), have complete access to the female students in all manner of undress.

The opposite is equally the case with homosexual male teachers supervising the locker rooms of male students. If heterosexual teachers of the opposite gender are barred from any access to partially clad students due to a presumption of unwelcome sexual attraction, then why should any less be true of *any* adults who share this attraction? However, instead of placing the needs of students first, schools have repeatedly swept this phenomenon under the rug, hoping that it will continue to elude the general public due to the inherent lack of political correctness that at the same time, has allowed this topic to remain hidden.

READ MORE FROM THE NEW YORK TIMES:

On the Web, Pedophiles Extend Their Reach

http://www.nytimes.com/2006/08/21/technology/21pedo.html?ei=5090&en=40a45848114deb35&ex=1313812800&partner=rssuserland&emc=rss&pagewanted=all

---

SOLUTION 53:

DISCONTINUE, AT ONCE, THE PRACTICE BY SCHOOLS OF PLACING ANY ADULTS IN THE POSITION OF OVERSEEING ANY MINOR CHILDREN IN ANY MANNER OF UNDRESS!

54.

TEACHERS CAN'T BE REASSIGNED
(IF THEY DON'T WANT TO BE)

Unlike a corporate manager, the school principal actually has very little control over the assignment of his/her staff members to the various position needs. Once a teacher is accorded a particular teaching assignment, particularly once a teacher is tenured; there is very little leeway in most union contracts to reassign a teacher to other responsibilities, regardless of need. While there is a little more flexibility within elementary schools, in that a 2nd grade teacher could find herself reassigned to the 5th grade the following year, they still could not be reassigned involuntarily. Further, a district could have too many teachers at the elementary school and not enough at the high school without having the power to compel teachers to relocate. This is also due, in part, to the specificity of teacher credentials that limit teachers to specific subject areas and grade levels. Still, a significant number of teachers are compensated at a higher pay rate for having obtained a master's degree, a degree often paid for by their school districts, only to subsequently refuse to use these new credentials that broaden their expertise to other teaching areas, with the school district's full sanction. This means that an English teacher who subsequently obtains a master's degree in special education or math can then refuse to fulfill one of these roles in lieu of keeping their same job, but at a higher salary due to their supplemental, (but unused), education.

There are hundreds of school districts all over America with multiple unfilled teaching positions in special education, math, science, and school administration, despite the fact that they already have teachers on their payroll who possess the needed credentials but who have opted to retain their less needed roles, while also continuing to enjoy annual raises and other benefits based on their subsequent acquisition of this additional schooling.

READ MORE FROM MIAMI, FLORIDA:

Teachers fight reassignment

http://www.miaminewsrecord.com/articles/2006/06/14/news/news1.txt

---

SOLUTION 54:

ELIMINATE EXTRA COMPENSATION TO TEACHERS WHO REFUSE TO UTILIZE THEIR GRADUATE TRAINING OR DEGREES.

55.

TEACHERS SHORTENED WORK YEAR - *PLUS* "PLANNING PERIODS"

Most working adults work year-round, work a full day, and are expected to achieve any work planning or preparation on their own time. Over 30 years since the enactment of equal employment laws empowering women's right to equal pay for equal work, leading to "working mothers" and "single mothers" no longer rare exceptions, school calendars are *still* designed around the premise of the two-parent, one wage-earner family. Fifty years ago it would have seriously disrupted America's family unit for children to be kept at school beyond mid-afternoon. How would they have time to help with the chores and enjoy Mom's home baked cookies? Further, expecting students to attend school during the summer months would have interfered with such tasks as helping with the planting and harvesting, and extended family vacations.

Teachers' shortened work year was also justified due to teachers having to be "on" all day instructing students, leaving little down time to plan a year's worth of lessons. Today, however, both the needs of families and teacher expectations have changed significantly. No longer are most parents at home in the middle of the afternoon, resulting in the kids being left to their own devices for a part of each day. Parents who opt to stay at home do so at great sacrifice to their careers and pocketbooks. Meanwhile, teachers are no longer required to teach during their entire workday. Instead, during a typical school schedule consisting of eight 50-minute class periods or intervals, most teachers only teach during five of these time segments, comprising just over four each day. One of the two or three remaining segments is used for lunch, and the other(s) their "planning" period(s). Apparently working two hours less each day than in most other occupations, as well as 3 months less each year *(with pay!)* is not sufficient time for them to "plan," even though most teach essentially the same lessons from year to year, even further minimizing this need for "planning." Not only that, would it not make sense for curriculum directors and other school administrators to do the planning to ensure lesson adherence with state and district learning goals? This, like many other school district decision, are made by America's school leaders without consulting their greatest benefactors, the American taxpayers.

READ MORE FROM THE NATIONAL CENTER FOR POLICY ANALYSIS:

Five myths about education

"In 2002, the average elementary school teacher made $30.75 per hour, which is a considerable amount when compared to other public servants, such as firefighters ($17.91) and police officers ($22.64)."

http://www.ncpa.org/sub/dpd/?page=article&Article_ID=2682

SOLUTION 55:

STOP PERMITTING "PLANNING PERIODS" FOR TEACHERS DURING THE SCHOOL DAY, DESIGNATING THIS TIME, AS NEEDED, TO THE LAST HOUR OF A TEACHER'S WORK DAY, (FROM 3 TO 4 P.M.) STILL ALLOWING THEM TO LEAVE WORK ONE FULL HOUR EARLIER THAN MOST OTHER AMERICAN WORKERS.)

56.

GUIDANCE COUNSELORS: TOO FEW FOR TOO MANY

Now that America's schools have become so fraught with emotionally-charged issues, from metal detectors to drug abuse, to gang wars, to teen pregnancies, most school guidance counselors are no longer adequately supported to handle the plethora of student problems. Most have caseloads of over 300 students for whom they are responsible for all class scheduling, transcript maintenance and college planning, leaving them barely enough time to meet with each student once per school year, let alone adequately address any of their serious emotional issues. Nevertheless, school leaders consistently fail to hire sufficient counselors to meet anything beyond their schools' recordkeeping needs, while student problems with anger, depression, bullying, conflict resolution, and school failure continue to multiply. Unlike 40 years ago, today in America there are a number of students who are attending school against their will or while being saddled with incredible obstacles to their success. Since American school laws require all students to attend school daily or else subject their parents to criminal penalties, there need to be sufficient supports in place to meet students' emotional, as well as instructional needs.

READ MORE FROM SAN RAFAEL, CALIFORNIA:

School counselors stretched thin-more jobs, lots more kids

http://www.usatoday.com/news/education/2004-05-27-school-counselors_x.htm

SOLUTION 56:

REQUIRE THAT NO MORE THAN 90 HIGH SCHOOL STUDENTS BE ASSIGNED TO ANY ONE SCHOOL COUNSELOR SO THAT IT IS FEASIBLE FOR EACH STUDENT TO BENEFIT FROM AT LEAST TWO MEANINGFUL COUNSELING SESSIONS PER SCHOOL YEAR TO EXPLORE ACADEMIC, CAREER, AND POST-SECONDARY EDUCATION OPTIONS.

57.

TEACHERS' AIDES:
THE LEAST-TRAINED TO DO THE MOST

"Teacher aides," "teacher assistants," and "paraprofessionals," are the most commonly used titles for the non-degreed individuals who work with one, a few, or a classroom of students with special learning needs, hired assist these students in accessing the instruction of the classroom teacher. Too often, however, the most difficult and under-performing students are assigned, almost exclusively, to these untrained and under-educated staff members. Instead of matching instructor skill level to students' particular exceptional needs, those with the least amount of professional academic training are often given the greatest responsibility for imparting instruction to students requiring the most specialized instruction. This is comparable to those with the greatest medical needs being treated not by their physicians trained in their particular medical specialty, but by one of the nurse's aides who changes their bedpans.

Even worse, more often than not, the schools fail to even utilize these individuals in the manner for which they are actually assigned. Most "aides" in a school are specifically hired to provide assistance to one or a group of students, as prescribed by these students' individualized special education plans, (IEPs). Instead, while some are accorded *all* instructional responsibility for these students, others are stuck making photocopies, grading papers, or performing other clerical duties for teachers who believe these school employees to be their personal assistants. Still, while not intended to either serve as teachers' private secretaries nor as students' teachers, most schools do not employ as many of these support staff members as their students actually need. In fact, many schools have been known to actually count them as being present in multiple classrooms simultaneously, or utilize one student's designated "one-on-one aide" to assist several other children, in violation of the students' mandated services. What only further complicates matters is that, in many school districts, these unskilled workers enjoy the same benefits of union membership as the more educated and credentialed teachers, a factor that can result in union-supported resistance to job assignments coupled with an imbalance of power between a long-employed and experienced "aide" and a brand new teacher or administrator.

READ MORE FROM THE NEBRASKA PROFESSIONAL PRACTICES COMMISSION:

STATE LAW REGARDING TEACHER AIDES

"The two major restrictions in the use of teacher aides are (1) aides may not be assigned teaching responsibilities, and (2) aides must be specifically prepared for their duties."

http://nppc.nol.org/aids.pdf#search='teacher%20aides%20unqualified'

SOLUTION 57:

UTILIZE AIDES AS FACILITATORS FOR STUDENTS WHO ARE THE MOST CAPABLE AND SELF-DIRECTED, WHILE PERMITTING THE HIGHLY-QUALIFIED TEACHERS TO DEVOTE THEIR EFFORTS TO THOSE WHO ARE LEAST CAPABLE.

THE FACILITIES:

"WHAT KIND OF PLACE IS THIS?"

58.

MOST SCHOOLS BUILDINGS CONTAIN MULTIPLE HAZARDS

Much has been written in recent years about the deplorable conditions in schools in some of the most destitute inner cites in America, from Harlem in New York, to Cabrini Green in Chicago, to East St. Louis, Illinois and beyond. But what is often not understood is how even schools in relatively "safe" neighborhoods may still contain numerous unsafe conditions that school officials are simply ignoring, either because few outsiders are aware of them, or because they cannot afford to make the needed repairs. Either way, there is frequently little sense of responsibility exhibited by school administrators toward notifying parents of the inherent dangers in their kids' schools.

Everything from dangling light fixtures to broken doors, to uneven stairs, to broken windows, to broken glass on the playgrounds, to brown water spewing from the drinking fountains, to broken and unsafe desks, to leaky toilets dripping to the classrooms below, to classrooms with such poor acoustics that the noise level is deafening, are simply all too common. The average elementary school has approximately 400 students and 100 staff members moving about, coming and going, using its facilities, each school day. The average high school has three or four times this amount. This causes wear and tear on floors, walls, and equipment. Facilities and equipment tend to break with frequent use. Unfortunately, whether from lack of resources or poor budgeting, the majority of schools are maintained in a manner that most would not tolerate in their own homes, or in any other places of business they regularly frequent, yet it is to these facilities where Americans are required to send their children each day, (or else pay dearly), while the schools' maintain a policy of never mentioning any such conditions to parents unless absolutely necessary.

To add to this travesty, there is no law in most states preventing students' exposure to dangerous mold, while asbestos removal and other demolition and reconstruction often takes place in schools during the school day with children present.

READ MORE FROM THE MASSACHUSETTS TEACHERS ASSOCIATION:

Inside MTA - (School) Environmental Hazards:

"Asbestos, Carpeting, Laboratory Safety, Molds, Multiple Chemical Sensitivity, Particulates, Pesticides, Radon, Volatile Organic Compounds"

http://www.massteacher.org/inside/ehs/hazards.cfm

SOLUTION 58:

HOLD SCHOOLS TO THE SAME STANDARDS OF SAFETY ACCORDED TO HOSPITALS AND OTHER PUBLIC FACILITIES.

59.

SCHOOL BATHROOMS: *UNFIT FOR PUBLIC USE*

In almost any public facility serving hundreds of individuals each day, the washrooms are serviced on an hourly basis to ensure that the facilities remain reasonably clean and sanitary. Not so in most of America's schools. Although literally hundreds of students may use the same toilets and sinks on any given day, no custodial maintenance occurs more than once each evening, with some schools even scaling this back to only once per week. This means bathrooms without toilet tissue or soap, while, at the same time, the school leaders would not dream of shortchanging their administrative salaries, treating its students and teachers like second-class citizens.

READ MORE FROM LOS ANGELES COUNTY, CA LEAGUE OF WOMEN VOTERS:

Are our schools healthy places?

http://www.smartvoter.org/1999nov/ca/la/vote/murphy_c/paper2.html

---

SOLUTION 59:

RECOGNIZE THE VOLUME OF WASHROOM USAGE IN SCHOOLS AND REQUIRE THAT THEY MAINTAIN A LEVEL OF CLENLINESS AT LEAST COMPATIBLE WITH MOST RESTAURANTS.

60.

NO AIR CONDITIONING!!!

Now, this particular topic may seem frivolous, and not really of significant concern. After all, early schools in America had no air conditioning and even most of America's "baby boomer" generation managed to complete 12 years of schooling without benefit of this luxury. Still, for this group the school year did not begin the third week of August nor remain in session until the third week of June, while also having large windows that could be opened as needed.

However, even as far north as Minneapolis, schools without air conditioning become virtual ovens in August. Little or no actual teaching or learning is able to occur under such conditions. School leaders know this, but hold school anyhow so as to allow enough days off during the school year and still meet their state's minimum attendance requirements. Additionally, many schools now hold summer school in non-air conditioned buildings knowing full well that effort is little more than an exercise in futility unless the humidity breaks. Nevertheless, almost without exception, the administrative offices of most schools *do* have ample air conditioning, which is one clear indicator of the priorities of the leadership.

It is the 21st Century. Asthma rates are on the rise. Students cannot learn and teachers cannot teach in stifling conditions. Lack of air conditioning when temperatures exceed 85 degrees is considered by the medical community to be a serious health hazard for most individuals. Few Americans would elect to spend seven hours attending a lecture, reading a book, or completing paperwork in a facility with 90 degree heat. How, then, can we expect our children to do so?

READ MORE FROM NEW HAVEN, CONNECTICUT:

WHEW!
Stifling weather empties schools

http://www.nhregister.com/site/news.cfm?newsid=14696239&BRD=1281&PAG=461&dept_id=517515&rfi=6

SOLUTION 60:

ESTABLISH "HUMAN COMFORT" STANDARDS FOR ALL SCHOOLS, AND DO NOT PERMIT ANY SCHOOL TO OPERATE WITHOUT AN INTERNAL TEMPERATURE RANGE OF MORE THAN 4 DEGREES ABOVE OR BELOW 72 DEGREES.

61.

SCHOOL BUSES: PARENTS' WORST NIGHTMARE

School buses should probably be outlawed. They exist primarily to counter free will and to assist schools in meeting their quotas, while being allowed to circumvent laws related to children's safety that would not be acceptable in any other setting. First, they create highly dangerous conditions by requiring children to stand outside, usually alone, to wait for a large vehicle that they must embark, without assistance, and without being struck by other cars, or worse. This vehicle is permitted to transport far more children than is reasonable, with the lone driver being assigned far more responsibility, than would be accorded an exceedingly more highly skilled teacher in a stationary classroom. Bus drivers are not required to have any particular training in supervising children, while the extent of criminal background checks and driving record verifications varies from one county to the next.

Even worse, while a private citizen can be cited if their own 6-year old is seat-belted into a bucket seat instead of a car seat, this same 6-year old child is legally permitted to ride a bench seat of a school bus, 15 feet from the supervision of the driver, with *no seat belt!* What's more, to control costs, students are often required to sit "three-to-a-seat" in bus seats only able to safely hold two students. Since the regulations allowing bus capacities did not consider the size of most students' backpacks, students who get stuck on the aisle often end up on the floor, guaranteeing that they will act as missiles if the bus makes any sudden stops.

Many schools, knowing of these unsafe conditions, have chosen to spend their money on video cameras mounted in the school buses in order to be able to capture school bus fights, rather than ensuring that each student is seated comfortably and safely.

READ MORE FROM CHICAGO:

Children and school bus dangers

http://www.halflifesource.com/site/news/children_and_school_bus_dangers/article6203.htm

---

SOLUTION 61:

REQUIRE THE SAME LEVEL OF CHILD SAFETY ON SCHOOL BUSES THAT ARE REQUIRED IN PRIVATE AUTOMOBILES, WHILE NEVER PERMITTING A CHILD TO RIDE IN UNSAFE CIRCUMSTANCES, OR WITH UNSAFE DRIVERS.

62.

SCHOOL LIBRARIES: IT'S NOT THE 50'S

There was a time when community libraries were a luxury that only the larger municipalities could afford. Books were expensive and difficult to obtain. School libraries served a valuable role in ensuring that students could access a broad number of books and other reading materials. This is simply no longer the case for most students today. Besides being expensive to keep stocked with the most current materials, most occupy far more space in today's' schools than the schools can actually afford. In most high schools, for example, students' required reading is limited to novels provided them by their teachers. Most research is conducted far more efficiently and accurately via the internet. Few students have the luxury of utilizing their school libraries to simply browse the shelves for a great book on their favorite topic or another by their favorite author. Even if they did, most school libraries usually are limited to very outdated sets of encyclopedias, an extensive set of Reader's Guides to Periodicals that almost no student has ever used, and a huge collection of fiction and non-fiction that dates back to the 60's and 70's, materials that are mostly for show, the majority having gone untouched by most of the students for decades. The cost to store and maintain these outdated materials does not justify the greater need for viable classroom space. Sure, students should continue to read the classics. However, most will only be compelled to do so when it is a class assignment, and then their school's library will likely only carry one or two copies, anyhow.

More and more students are opting, instead, for frequenting one of the local bookstore chains that are cropping up everywhere, along with their far more up-to-date community libraries. This is not such a bad thing, and illustrates one need America's schools no longer need to struggle to fulfill.

READ MORE FROM BURLINGTON COUNTY, PA:

Board rules outdated books in school libraries should go

http://www.phillyburbs.com/pb-dyn/news/112-08182004-350288.html

---

SOLUTION 62:

UTILIZE CURRENT SCHOOL LIBRARY SPACE TO REDUCE OVER-CROWDED CLASSROOMS, PARTNER WITH LOCAL LIBRARIES TO ARRANGE REGULAR STUDENT VISITS, WHILE PROVIDING STUDENTS GREATER OPPORTUNITIES TO ACCESS AND CONDUCT RESEARCH.

63.

SCHOOL LOCKER ROOMS: IT'S NOT THE 60'S

Another potential area of wasted space is the typically oversized locker room and shower area present in most high school lockers. In this age of enlightened sexual identity, coupled with greater potential for sexual harassment, most schools no longer encourage their students to shower in the presence of other students, a rather humiliating and sometimes barbaric practice most parents remember with a shudder. Right or wrong, the exercise level most students attain in P.E. class today does not compel them to shower, nor are more students permitted sufficient time in which to do so. Typically, the only time anyone showers at school is following an especially grueling football game, and then usually only the players covered in too much mud and blood to get into their cars will not wait to shower when they get home. Two or three single shower stalls should suffice.

READ MORE FROM CHULA VISTA, CA

Where have all the showers gone?

http://www.csmonitor.com/2004/0203/p12s01-legn.html

SOLUTION 63:

REHABILITATE LARGE SHOWER AREAS PRESENT IN MOST HIGH SCHOOLS AS WORK OUT ROOMS FOR STUDENTS WHO PREFER LESS ORGANIZED PHYSICAL ACTIVITY.

64.

SCHOOL COMPUTER LABS: IT'S NOT THE 70'S

Today, almost every school has a "computer lab," meaning they have one classroom dedicated to rows of computers situated at each of 20 to 30 desks. However, just as the school library is largely for show, this facility, as well, is not as readily available to students as outsiders might imagine. It is typically shared by the entire school, meaning that students are only brought to the lab on certain days, by certain teachers, to complete certain assignments. Only rarely are students allowed to access computerized enhancements of their lessons on a regular basis, or to conduct independent research. Their access to all of the knowledge they could ever need is largely stifled during the school day. Today, in order to actually bring American education to the 21st century, all students should be afforded their own computer stations at school where they can access needed information at will. Anything less, in terms of computer lab usage, merely gives schools the appearance of being technologically progressive than actually serving to prepare students for the future. Currently, the shortage of qualified teachers is staggering and only continues to grow. How simple it would be, then, to allow those students most adept at computerized instruction to pursue their own learning at times while teachers rotated their teaching, thereby providing each student more individualized instruction.

READ MORE FROM THE KENTUCKY DEPARTMENT OF EDUCATION:

Should School Computer Labs Be Phased Out?

"Computers belong in all classrooms, not held captive in the computer lab and taught as a specialized subject area at a scheduled time."

http://www.education.ky.gov/NR/rdonlyres/eliqizgunsnemjt76xbkiwn6fnxpw5wtyxogq7mxhjoozqvjop6wcs6pi675fazlen37iylls6oafjvz2xv3cconfub/labvsclass.pdf#search='computers%20do%20not%20belong%20in%20labs'

SOLUTION 64:

EITHER TAKE THE COMPUTERS OUT OF "LABS" AND INTO STUDENTS' CLASSROOMS, OR ELSE MAKE THESE COMPUTER STATIONS AVAILABLE TO STUDENTS THROUGHOUT THE SCHOOL DAY, AS NEEDED.

65.

NO SCHOOL "PREMISES LIABILITY"

Any parent would hope that anyone with whom they entrust their children's care would exercise sufficient concern and responsibility to ensure their safety and well being. It would also be hoped that sufficient laws are in place to hold those accountable who should fail in this responsibility. It would probably surprise most parents, then, to learn that schools, not unlike other government municipalities, are considered *exempt* from any premises liability. Apparently, this law was originally enacted to protect government offices from being unduly sued to the point of being no longer able to serve the public. However, we are not talking about the Post Office or the Department of Motor Vehicles, just two of many government offices that individuals enter *voluntarily*. We are talking about public schools, where parents are required by law to send their children each and every day. Unfortunately, while kids are injured every day in schools by unsafe equipment, facility mismanagement and inadequate supervision by teachers and other school staff, schools are required to assume no risk of liability. This is just wrong. Period.

In most states, schools attempt to sell parents supplemental "accident insurance," to cover the students while at school, and to offset this lack of professional responsibility. While the schools' commissions on these policies is not known, it is just one more clear example of faulty school logic; requiring parents to pay for protection from the schools' shortcomings.

READ MORE FROM A HOBART, INDIANA SCHOOL HANDBOOK:

SCHOOL LIABILITY AND STUDENT ACCIDENTS

"Each year the school has a problem with misunderstanding about financial responsibility for medical treatment of students who are injured while in the regular school program. In such cases, parents wrongfully assume that expenses caused by these injuries will be paid by the school or by insurance carried by the school corporation. The school corporation does not carry student accident insurance nor does it pay bills to doctors or others for treatment of injuries incurred by students. This is a responsibility of the parent."

http://www.hobart.k12.in.us/ge/handbook/liabilit.html

SOLUTION 65:

HOLD ALL SCHOOLS ACCOUNTABLE FOR THE SAFETY OF THEIR STUDENTS TO ENSURE THEIR SUFFICIENT ATTENTION TO THEIR STUDENTS' WELL-BEING AT ALL TIMES.

THE INSTRUCTION

"HOW COULD THEY?"

66.

NO INSTRUCTIONAL CONSISTENCY

Despite the great disparity in schools from one region to the next, there are some common terms and labels that are used consistently throughout virtually all of America's schools, such as "the Third Grade," "Algebra Class," and "the Letter Grades A through F." So, although a number of school procedures and practices are modified by local school boards to suit local student needs, there remains an overriding belief by most Americans that the basic tenets of public education are consistent and grounded in some common understanding. Not only is this not the case from district to district, it is often equally not true from school to school or from classroom to classroom in *the same district.*

What constitutes a passing grade, for example, is still today largely subjective. While each school district may prescribe and publish their grading policies of 90% or above equals an "A," 80% to 89% equals a "B," and so on, the percentage points that go into these formulas, as well as the allocations of points for each assignment, are left completely to each teacher's discretion, and are almost never challenged. That means, then, that two students could easily earn far different grades for identical work from two different teachers of the same subject within the same school. This can be due to differences in teaching styles, differences in subject interpretation, as well as differences in teachers' grading policies, particularly where one teacher allows a student's behavior to influence their overall grade, while another does not. Classroom behavior, while a factor in students' capacities to learn, are far too often used to penalize students for factors having absolutely nothing to do with their acquisition of the required material. Their grades may be reduced for such offenses as tardiness, late work, or speaking out of turn. In turn, students with similar performance may actually receive a higher grade for factors unrelated to learning, as well, including their manners, degree of neatness, or for punctuality. In a fervent attempt at compelling student conformity, (which is often deemed necessary to successfully convey instruction to 25 or 30 students at one time), most teachers have resorted to blackmailing students by withholding grade points for noncompliance to garner their full cooperation. Despite the fact that nowhere in any federal or state learning goals for any subject area is there any mention of changing or improving students' behavior, teachers are, nevertheless, allowed to blatantly withhold or lower grade points of students who misbehave, while also "confusing" compliance as academic achievement, when it is in no way a factor in students' *academic* growth.

Letter grades, therefore, are virtually meaningless, as are grade levels. Classes of students with huge learning and performance differences are regularly "promoted" to the next grade level with identical labels of academic achievement, namely their new "grade levels." Most educators involved with this practice tell themselves they are doing what's best for the students. Much has been publicized suggesting that there are few, if any, benefits to retaining a student, (e.g. "failing," "flunking," or being "held back,"), with research indicating far more long-range negative effects. This may or may not be the case, since there is no way to know the fate of the students studied had they *not* been "promoted" without sufficient academic preparation. Further, these studies all examined strictly the practice of reassigning students with those who are younger, resulting in public humiliation and shame. This is neither sensible nor logical. At the same time, it makes absolutely no sense to promote a student and then subject him or her to an elaborate scheme of deception where everyone involved simply *pretends* that the student can master the prescribed work of the next grade level, when it is clear that they have yet to master the work from the previous grade!

Further, it is scientifically impossible to expect that all children born within an artificially created "grade year," will be at the same developmental level as all others born within these parameters, or that they will all be at the same performance level in all subjects at the same time. Even back in the day of the one-room schoolhouse teachers understood and accommodated this phenomenon better that most schools do today. Having all grade-levels in one classroom, a student would be allowed to move ahead by *subject,* not by age or date on the calendar, and only when they actually *mastered* the given material.

READ MORE FROM THE WASHINGTON POST:

Algebra = X in One School, Y in Another: Teaching Inconsistent as Standards Waver

http://www.fairness.com/resources/one?resource_id=46 14

SOLUTION 66:

ELIMINATE ARBITRARY LETTER GRADES AND GRADE LEVELS, AND INSTEAD HOLD STUDENTS AND TEACHERS ACCOUNTABLE ONLY TO SPECIFIC EDUCATIONAL BENCHMARKS ESTABLISHED FOR EACH SUBJECT AREA.

67.

TOO MUCH INSTRUCTIONAL CONTENT LEFT TO TEACHERS' DISCRETION

Continuing the theme of "instructional inconsistency," America's teachers are permitted far too much latitude in deciding what they will and will not teach. This is not entirely their fault. State learning goals are, for the most part, unbelievably vague, while most school district curricula are often limited to the names of text books. Teachers are expected to apply their own abilities as teachers to impart the required skills and knowledge to their students as they see fit. What's missing is the diagnostic determination of each individual student's present skills and levels of understanding that is then matched to a prescribed instructional "protocol." Instead, due to the disparate skill levels of many of the students, much of the material is not covered sufficiently for them to grasp the required concepts. Further, the disparity between teaching styles is not at all matched to student needs, only to school scheduling needs. One teacher may give only multiple-choice tests, for example, while another requires strictly essays. Further, teachers' work performance is neither measured nor evaluated on their ability to adhere consistently to state learning goals. Further, there is almost never any comparison of students' performance on standardized tests and which teacher they had for the given subjects, to determine if some teachers actually are doing a better job.

Teachers perform their jobs largely in a vacuum, removed from any scrutiny or supervision by the principal or other administrator. Most teachers' union contracts require that administrative observations of their performance be limited to two times per year, always with advance warning, and generally for not more than 50 minutes. During these "formal observations" the teacher will instruct a very carefully prepared lesson to students who have often been coached to perform in a superior manner. The administrator almost always limits their assessment to qualities related to the teacher's personality and classroom management, such as "eye contact," "variance of instructional method," "written preparation," and "organization." Because the evaluating administrator is frequently not familiar with the particular tenets of the subject area being taught, little or no consideration is given to the accuracy or quality of the instruction, or to its compatibility with state mandated goals. What is also not considered is the teacher's skill at adapting the instruction for any students with special learning needs. Quality of daily assignments, assessment of student learning, and the teacher's grading practices are all but ignored.

READ MORE FROM THE WISCONSIN CENTER FOR EDUCATIONAL RESEARCH:

<u>Measuring the Content of Instruction</u>
"Classroom teachers are the ultimate arbiters of what is taught, and how."
http://www.wcer.wisc.edu/news/coverStories/measuring_content_instruction.php

---

SOLUTION 67:

DE-EMPHASIZE TEACHER EVALUATIONS BASED ON BRIEF CLASSROOM OBSERVATIONS, AND, INSTEAD, PLACE GRATER EMPHASIS ON ACTUAL TEACHER OUTCOMES.

68.

NO GRADE-TO-GRADE ARTICULATION

Besides there being significant inconsistencies in the instruction of the same material between teachers at the same grade level, what is even more disturbing is how these inconsistencies are carried over from one grade to the next with compounding consequences. There is rarely any discussion between teachers from one grade level to the next regarding students' instructional or learning needs. At best, teachers may get together at the end of the school year to briefly address certain students' *behavioral* concerns, but rarely academic ones. For one thing, few teachers are willing to admit when they failed to teach a student everything that was required of them. (Besides, since no one else is checking on this, why should they admit to it?) Whenever a student does fail to achieve, teachers almost always blame the students' parents, culture, socioeconomic level, a "disability," or else society in general. *IT IS NEVER THE TEACHER'S FAULT!*

In no other successful business operation anywhere is one step in a multi-step process permitted to function completely independently from all of the other parts, with so little accountability for the final product. Once a student is "passed" from one teacher to the next, the receiving teacher almost never communicates with the previous teachers about the student, nor do the prior teachers ever learn anything of the outcomes of the students whom they "passed." One way to avoid this would be to start requiring "admission tests" to determine a student's capacity for entrance into the next grade level for each subject area. This would not mean that any students failing to pass these criteria should necessarily be retained with younger students, but instructed, *with their same-aged peers,* only at the academic level that matches their current levels of academic achievement.

> **READ MORE FROM LEARNING POINT ASSOCIATES:**
>
> **A Lack of Communication, Articulation, and Alignment of Goals and Philosophies Between the Different Schools in the District**
>
> http://www.ncrel.org/sdrs/areas/issues/content/cntareas/math/ma4lack.htm

---

SOLUTION 68:

REQUIRE THAT SCHOOLS UTILIZE STUDENTS' STANDARDIZED TEST SCORES TO DETERMINE STUDENTS' READINESS TO MOVE TO THE NEXT LEVEL OF INSTRUCTION FOR EACH SUBJECT AREA.

69.

"SCHEDULED THINKING"

Another problem with America's schools that was actually *created* by the current school format is the concept of "incremental learning." With the growing pressure to cram more subjects into a given school day, coupled with the elevated status of a number of originally "non-essential" teachers, every subject in a student's schedule must be given equal time, resulting in students being required to switch gears from literature, to biology, to ancient history, to volleyball, to geometry, for only 45 minute increments, and that's just before lunch! Who among us can actually learn anything substantial in this manner? Add to this the fact that students who were simply "passed" to the next "grades" during their developmental years are now ill-equipped to process this new information at this pace, nor are most able to demonstrate sufficient understanding.

Think back to any time in your life when you needed to accomplish something of any significance and length, be it planning a wedding, rebuilding a carburetor, weeding the garden, organizing the family photos, teaching your child to ride their bike, or rewriting a company manual. Would anyone choose to limit one's time for any of these tasks to 45 minutes? Further still, would anyone be willing to try to spend 45 minutes on each of these activities in one day and expect any of them to be done well? Granted, this schedule is not so dissimilar to that of a mother of small children, although even she has the luxury of controlling her own distribution of her time. *No one* would volunteer for this lengthy and uninterrupted sequence of tasks, with no control over their use of time, being treated as captive slaves, not being permitted to leave a given room or even one's seat without fear of punishment or loss of status.

There is reportedly a marked increase in the number of diagnosed cases of Attention-deficit Hyperactivity Disorder, of ADHD in America. Could it be that America's schools, in their zeal to bombard students with multiple subject matter being delivered each hour, (each subject requiring completely different and unrelated abilities and skills), actually be *creating* this condition in children by compelling such unnatural responses to such varying stimuli?

Even colleges and universities, whose students have demonstrated at least some level of intellectual superiority in order to gain admission, (in most cases), realize that this format does not serve to maximize one's capacity to learn, and so allow their students to set their own schedules, while also discouraging the scheduling of more than three different subjects in one day. This practice would seem even more valid with even younger students.

READ MORE FROM THE UNIVERSITY OF MICHIGAN:
Is your child overscheduled & overstressed? U-M expert offers tips on how to tell — and what to do

http://www.med.umich.edu/opm/newspage/2005/hmchildstress.htm

SOLUTION 69:
USE MORE STUDENT-DIRECTED LEARNING THAT ALLOWS STUDENTS MORE FREEDOM AND FLEXIBILITY TO PROGRESS IN SUBJECT AREAS AT THEIR OWN PACE, PERMITTING THEM MORE TIME FOR THOUGHTFUL REFLECTION; RATHER THAN FORCING THEM TO INGEST A MARATHON OF INSTRUCTION IN MULTIPLE SUBJECTS EACH AND EVERY DAY.

70.

NO "LIGHT AT THE END OF THE TUNNEL"

Much of the failure of America's schools in recent years has been largely attributed to students' bad behavior. This is largely accurate. Many students are highly frustrated with being trapped in a backwards and antiquated system that still views teachers as the keepers of all knowledge, when nothing could be further from the truth. Practically *all* knowledge, (not to be confused with the acquisition of *skills)*, can, today, be acquired by students via far more masterful and effective means. Several educational television channels, for example, are devoted solely to providing comprehensive, factual, and easily understood information on virtually every topic in history, physics, biology, and literature. Further, almost every American student alive today has had at least some experience with perusing the Internet to locate information on a myriad of subjects. Teachers' unwavering practice of droning on in a far less skilled or illustrative lecture format about a single topic, knowing that their students could access the information themselves, is what is driving many of today's students crazy! What egos we have as Americans to believe that a heavily researched million-dollar production on World War II broadcast on the History Channel, compiled by a litany of brilliant scholars and videographers, would not compare to the interpretation of this event by one lowly teacher with a bachelor's degree in social science. As teacher shortages grow only more critical, America continually fails to fully utilize one of its cheapest and most readily available instructional resources, video programming, simply out of some misplaced need to cling to the "traditional classroom" format.

But, by and large, what frustrates many students more than anything else is their teachers' unilateral control of the unknown. This is primarily the case in two areas; knowledge of what the next assignment will be, and knowledge of students' class grades. Teachers tend to hold these two pieces of information close to their vests, much to the irritation of many students old enough to understand and need regular feedback. They both want to know what lies ahead and also where their performance stands at any given time. Much off-task behavior and lack of student motivation could be easily alleviated, by simply making students, even young students, aware of where they stand and what comes next in terms of assignment expectations.

Studies of postal workers, known for their higher-than-average percentage of mental breakdowns and propensity for violence, have shown that this phenomenon is primarily attributable to the steady and unending stream of new mail, without any breaks, and regardless of how effectively they handled the previous batch. This is how many students feel, as well. What most teachers fail to consider is how frustrating it is for a student to labor over a research paper or expository essay, while having no knowledge whether the same or similar assignment is awaiting them around the next bend the following week. Providing a list of all of the assignments for an entire semester, for example, provides many students an enormous sense of relief at being able to know in advance exactly what is to be expected of them. Further, having ongoing knowledge of one's progress in each subject relieves much anxiety, while also informing students both of their accomplishments as well as how much more they need to achieve in order to be successful. Colleges know this and so require their instructors to provide students a syllabus for all of their classes, yet America's elementary and high schools have, nevertheless, failed to adopt this proven practice.

READ MORE FROM THE UNIVERSITY OF DELAWARE:

WHAT MAKES INSTRUCTION EFFECTIVE FOR US?

http://cte.udel.edu/TAbook/voices.htm

SOLUTION 70:

REQUIRE TEACHERS TO REVEAL SPECIFIC COURSE REQUIREMENTS AND ASSIGNMENTS TO STUDENTS AT THE BEGINNING OF EACH TERM.

71.

"LATE" WORK IS PENALIZED:
BUT IT'S STILL LEARNING

While on the subject of late work, here's one more concept for America's parents to watch out for: *"Getting what you pay for."* If, as adults, we signed up and paid for a class and then had a personal life complication causing us a delay in submitting our homework, we would still expect to be able to submit it late for at least partial credit, right? Well, lest it's been forgotten, America's students (and their parents) are also *paying customers* and so should receive no less consideration. America's schools so often appear to forget the actual origin of their financial capital: American tax dollars. Even though there are some students who do not happen to be the children of taxpayers, America's citizens still have to pay for any of these students' resulting school failures, one way or another, and so need for them, like all students in America, to be provided every opportunity to succeed. Ironically, what most educators don't realize is that by overusing their authority to penalize students with lowered grades for late work they are actually creating more student failures, resulting in far less favorable NCLB outcomes for their schools.

READ MORE FROM THE LEARNING RESOURCES NETWORK (LERN), RIVER FALLS, WISCONSIN:

SMART BOYS, BAD GRADES
http://www.smartboysbadgrades.com/tips4teachers.htm

SOLUTION 71:

STOP PENALIZING STUDENTS FOR "LATE WORK," IF THEY HAVE DEMONSTRATED SUFFICIENT MASTERY WITHIN THE PRESCRIBED GRADING PERIOD.

72.

SUBJECT KNOWLEDGE DOES NOT GUARANTEE AN ABILITY TO TEACH

One of the greatest flaws with America's present school system is the way in which it trains its teachers. While it would not be expected that simply someone who merely studied kidneys could perform kidney surgery, someone with a degree in Biology, for example, is expected to know how to impart this knowledge to students with only one "methods" course and some supervised "student teaching." The one course on how to actually teach the subject matter is often focused primarily on student projects, wherein equally inexperienced classmates take turns developing and presenting their "lessons" on their given subject to the rest of their college student classmates, rather than to any group of students for whom the lessons were actually designed. Little actual practical knowledge or experiences are provided the teacher trainees regarding means of ensuring student learning. Further, there is no requirement that teacher trainees actually be able to demonstrate an ability to *teach* something to someone, before being released to America's schools to call themselves "teachers."

"Student teaching," consisting of one semester, in which a teacher trainee shadows a working teacher, usually includes very little original, teacher-trainee-developed or delivered instruction. The teacher is graded primarily on likeability cooperation, and "classroom management," not whether the student subjects demonstrate any actual academic gains. Of course, there are problems associated with using student subjects for teacher "practice." Still, as with the medical field, "Teaching Schools," like "Teaching Hospitals" could be established that students in which students could be enrolled voluntarily. Further, unlike subjecting a patient to multiple surgeries, being exposed to extra instruction would hardly seem to have many negative consequences.

READ MORE FROM THE DONALDSON LEARNING PROJECT, LYME CONNECTICUT:

WHAT'S WRONG WITH OUR ED SCHOOLS?

"Simply enough, most of our schools of education do not teach prospective teachers how to teach. Or, put another way, how to create classrooms where students learn what they should be learning."

http://www.brainsarefun.com/Edschools.html

SOLUTION 72:

REQUIRE THAT COLLEGES AND UNIVERSITIES INCLUDE MORE SPECIFIC INSTRUCTIONAL TECHNIQUES IN TEACHER TRAINING, UTILIZING REAL STUDENT SUBJECTS.

73.

QUASHED NATURAL TENDANCIES: WORK, MARRIAGE, PARENTING

Throughout the entire history of mankind until the mid 20th century, individuals in their late teens naturally were drawn to find permanent partners, to marry, and to begin supporting themselves and their own households and raise their families. This was both expected and supported by American society since the first settlers. Somehow, however, in America's quest to beat Russia in the space program, or to surpass Japan in mathematical achievement, or other achieve other lofty goals, Americans not only lost sight of this option as a viable direction for some young people, it was all but done away with entirely. Americans have now, somehow, come to expect *every* young adult to suddenly be capable of suppressing their natural desires and to postpone all thoughts of young love or tendency toward "settling down." Any American high school student expressing such an interest today is made to feel as though they are giving up bigger and better opportunities, while failing to aspire to their full potential. Unfortunately, by discouraging all young adults from acknowledging their natural tendencies toward commitment and being responsible for their own families, some may be less compelled to enter into permanent commitments, while being more likely to abandon their parental responsibilities, in the future. Further, in having been "rerouted" from their quest for early dual self-sufficiency, while, instead, continuing their dependence on parents and others well into early adulthood, some may be more likely to become involved in drugs, gangs, or other criminal behavior as they seek substitutes for their needs for attachment and autonomy. Being held solely responsible for the care of their spouses and children, many might, instead, avoid these choices altogether.

America's schools lead the nation's crusade of suppressing adult tendencies by perpetuating the treatment of physical adults as children far beyond what is either necessary or mentally healthy. Future historians may bemoan how are Americans are now affecting the natural order by never meeting their great-grandchildren who will now be born long after they die or are too old to impact their lives. How Americans are affecting future generations by erasing all evidence of teenagers being capable of running their own lives, by marrying, being heads of their own nuclear families, or responsible parents, remains to be seen. Of course, these choices, as well, are not appropriate for all students. Nevertheless, there is a direct correlation between the increase in gangs, drugs, and violence and the imposed mandatory years of school attendance, and other laws that all but criminalize early self-sufficiency.

READ MORE FROM WOMEN'S HEALTH NEWS:

Schools failing to support teens who are pregnant or new mothers

http://www.news-medical.net/?id=793

SOLUTION 73:

REQUIRE THAT SCHOOLS RECOGNIZE AND RESPECT MANY YOUNG ADULTS' NATURAL PROGRESSION TOWARD ADULT RESPONSIBILITIES AND RELATIONSHIPS AND DO NOT IN ANY WAY CHASTISE OR IMPAIR THEIR DECISIONS, WHILE ALSO SUPPORTING THEIR NEED TO COMBINE THEIR ADULT ROLES WITH COMPLETING THEIR EDUCATION.

74.

LEARNING AT ONE'S OWN PACE = PUNISHMENT

America's Schools expect groups of students, born during prescribed 12-month period, to progress at equal rates, in *all* subject areas, throughout their academic careers. If a student should happen to fall behind in one particular subject area they are treated punitively by their schools by being accorded negative grades. If they happen to achieve beyond their peers, they are not permitted to work ahead, only to continue to endure the instruction meant for their less-achieving classmates, with no reduction in the amount of required "busywork," while experiencing little or no new learning until the rest of the class catches up.

READ MORE FROM THE NATIONAL EDUCATION COMMISSION ON TIME AND LEARNING:
The design flaw

"Decades of school improvement efforts have foundered on a fundamental design flaw, the assumption that learning can be doled out by the clock and defined by the calendar."

http://members.tripod.com/h_javora/design_flaw.htm

SOLUTION 74:

ELIMINATE BIRTHDATES AS A DETERMINING FACTOR IN STUDENTS' CLASS PLACEMENTS, INSTEAD BASING THESE PLACEMENTS ON EACH STUDENT'S CURRENT LEVEL OF MEASURED ACADEMIC ACHIEVEMENT IN EACH SUBJECT AREA.

75.

STUDENTS' OWN INTERESTS NOT PART OF THE "LESSON PLAN"

Before there was formal schooling, children and teenagers naturally gravitated toward their areas of strongest interest or need, and these would become their adult vocations. Today, however, if a student has a particular interest, they are not permitted to pursue it unless it fits into their school's curriculum, and then only during prescribed times. For example, no matter how much a student may enjoy studying ancient history or poetry, doing painting or woodworking, learning computer programming or child psychology, if instruction in these disciplines is only offered during one semester of the student's junior year of high school, then that's all they get. If students have strong interests in subject areas not offered by their schools, such as anthropology, world religions, or Greek mythology, again, that's too bad. All natural tendencies toward learning have now become programmed and institutionalized. What might American schools be doing to alter future generations, in fact, the future of mankind, by continuing to quash its future artists, poets, philosophers, and explorers?

READ MORE FROM WASHINGTON, D.C.:
Incorporating Student Voice into Teaching Practice.
"Acknowledging the importance of student voice in the classroom means acknowledging students' active role in the learning process."
http://www.ericdigests.org/2000-4/voice.htm

SOLUTION 75:

ALLOW STUDENTS GREATER INSTRUCTIONAL CHOICE AND STOP REQUIRING THEM TO STUDY PRIMARLY SUBJECTS FOR WHICH THEY HAVE LITTLE INTEREST.

76.

"TEACHING" = (MERELY) "PRESENTING"

With most class sizes in America's schools generally hovering around 30 students, with teachers being required to instruct a new subject, and sometimes a new group of students every 45 minutes or so, little actual "teaching" is able to take place, only presenting. This is the reason why so many private tutoring companies are thriving in America today. In order to ensure that their children receive any real *teaching*, many parents in America have resorted to purchasing outside instructional services to supplement what their children are not receiving from their schools. This only underscores the futility of America's schools continuing to fail to utilize the extensive teaching resources that are already readily available to them. Far more students could be instructed more effectively in a broad number of subjects, in a far more comprehensive manner, via instructional video and software productions already produced in virtually every topic required by all federal and state learning goals. Most of today's students are far more accustomed to learning via this method, anyhow, which, if utilized, could also serve to reduce the number of student behavioral and motivational problems.

READ MORE FROM

THE UNIVERSITY OF VIRGINIA:

Reconcilable Differences? Standards-Based Teaching and Differentiation.

http://www.ascd.org/ed_topics/el200009_tomlinson.htm 1

SOLUTION 76:

INCORPORATE MORE OPPORTNITIES FOR STUDENT-DIRECTED INSTRUCTION INSTEAD OF STUDENTS BEING COMPLETELY DEPENDENT UPON THEIR OVER-EXTENDED TEACHERS. ENCOURAGE MORE TEACHERS TO ACCESS "STATE OF THE ART" INSTRUCTION FOR THEIR STUDENTS, WHILE DEVOTING MORE OF THEIR INDIVIDUAL INSTRUCTION TO THOSE WHO ACTUALLY NEED IT.

77.

PE: A HUGE WASTE OF TIME & TEACHERS

President Kennedy had a good idea. Children need to adopt and maintain active lifestyles. Most do. They play little league, flag football, soccer, basketball, and hockey. They do ballet, gymnastics, cheerleading, and baton twirling. There are park districts programs, YMCA programs, neighborhood leagues, city leagues, and church leagues. Very few children in America have *no* access to regular and frequent exercise. With rising school costs and growing teacher shortages, it is, therefore, highly unnecessary for any school monies to be wasted on programs that can be more easily delivered and managed by those with recreation and sports backgrounds, but not necessarily teaching degrees, while remembering schools' first obligation is to teach academics. There are already procedures in place to allow for school waivers for such external programs as private driver training and music lessons, while most high school athletes are also accorded "P.E. waivers." It is certainly feasible, then, for schools to simply require students to provide documentation of their participation in after-school physical activities, which would also serve to provide more community jobs, fulfill more childcare needs, while also keeping more kids off the streets.

Since studies have shown that far more children today are overweight than was true in the 1960's, it is time to try a different approach to Kennedy's ideal. Instead of 45 minutes of daily "P.E." classes, rarely consisting of any true or sustained exercise, while interrupting more focused academics, students could, instead, participate in regular daily or weekly activities of extended length designed to promote both sportsmanship and physical well-being. Meanwhile, America's highly paid P.E. "teachers" could apply their teaching credentials in one of the much needed teacher shortage areas.

READ MORE FROM NASHVILLE, TENNESSEE:

So just how bad is your child's gym class?

"P.E. programs often poorly run, provide few health benefits."

http://www.newsweek.co.uk/id/6835788/

SOLUTION 77:

RECOGNIZE THAT "PHYSICAL" EDUCATION IS NOT A TRUE ACADEMIC DISCIPLINE BUT SIMPLY A MEANS OF KEEPING KIDS PHYSICALLY ACTIVE, AND STOP ACCORDING IT EQUAL IMPORTANCE.

78.

"CHEATING" vs. MAKING LEARNING EASY

Although teachers are often under extreme pressure to teach kids an extensive list of prescribed material within a rather short timeframe, they will, nevertheless, go out of their way to make sure that kids never learn anything the easy way. Generally, any method that allows students to absorb information too easily is perceived as "cheating," as though the final instructional objective is something other than the students learning and remembering the material by whatever means. Every advertising campaign in the world takes advantage of tried and true methods of using clever phrases, colorful visuals, memorable rhythms, and frequent repetition to teach the unsuspecting public anything and everything. Still, many teachers resist any similar techniques to ensure that their students learn. There is a category of teaching materials, used only rarely by most teachers, called "high interest." The methods employed by these tools, primarily relating the material to something more familiar, or adapting it to catchy tunes, are typically avoided by instructors as being "too easy." Somewhere along the way, instead of learning being a pleasurable and enjoyable experience, educators decided that it needed to be drudgery in order for it to really "count." *(Perhaps to justify their jobs?)*

As a result, kids who are able to memorize large quantities of useless material, including rap lyrics, advertising jingles, and sports statistics, are somehow unable to draw from these same abilities to memorize the Pythagorean Theorem, the Periodic Table of Elements, or the Bill of Rights.

The reality is that kids have absolutely no trouble learning anything they need to know to navigate their own world. Adults, in general, and teachers, in particular, need to stop worrying so much about exerting their authority over kids and, instead, start trying to relate to them. Perhaps if more teachers would try to relate their lessons to their students' lives, more students would actually learn more easily. The reality is that if teachers could reduce their class sizes by being able to pass on each student who demonstrated a level of subject mastery, instead of keeping them for the rest of the year, more real teaching would likely occur. Further, by teachers building more positive and less punitive relationships with their students they would naturally create for them more bridges to their successful adulthood.

READ MORE FROM THE UNIVERSITY OF OREGON:

Why Teachers Do Not Use Collaborative/Cooperative Learning

http://tep.uoregon.edu/resources/librarylinks/articles/nousecooplearn.html

---

SOLUTION 78:

INCORPORATE INTO TEACHING MORE WAYS IN WHICH MOST CHILDREN ACTUALLY LEARN AND STOP WITHHOLDING METHODS THAT ACTUALLY WORK OUT OF A MISPLACED FEAR THAT SCHOOL MIGHT BECOME TOO MUCH "FUN."

79.

IRRESPONSIBLE INSTRUCTION

There is, in virtually every curricula being taught in America's schools today, some degree of ill-advised, inaccurate, or misguided instruction. There are lessons that only tell one side of a war, only examine one race's ancestry, or one nation's perspective of world events. There are irresponsible science teachers who regularly conduct experiments wherein students are shown that they can drink Drano when they mix it with hydrochloric acid, or that they can make helium "bombs" by lighting helium balloons on fire. There are countless English teachers who regularly use improper English, foreign language teachers who use secondary dialects, and math teachers who allow students to rely too heavily on calculators without ever ensuring their understanding of basic operations.

Most textbooks used in America's schools are chock full of irresponsible and biased information. A monopoly of only a very few publishers, mostly from Texas, supply the textbooks used in the majority of America's schools. While some efforts have been made to eliminate much of the "political incorrectness," much subjective bias still remains.

Nevertheless, unlike any other professional services, teaching bears virtually no risk of malpractice claims. Teachers remain protected from any responsibility for students' cognitive injuries resulting from their classes, while their teaching remains completely shielded from any comparison to their actual students' performance on State tests. (A school's math scores are never further identified by particular math teacher, for example.)

READ MORE FROM EDUCATION WEEK:

Why so many underqualified high school teachers?

http://www.teaching-point.net/Exhibit%20A/Underqualified%20High%20School%20Teachers.pdf#search='TEACHERS%20TEACHING%20LIES'

SOLUTION 79:

HOLD TEACHERS AND SCHOOL LEADERS PERSONALLY ACCOUNTABLE FOR IMPARTING GROSS MIS-INFORMATION OR FAULTY INSTRUCTION THAT LEADS TO COGNITIVE, EMOTIONAL, OR PHYSICAL HARM.

80.

HOMEWORK: SCHOOLS' ULTIMATE INTRUSION

One of the most intrusive practices into family life by America's schools is the concept of "homework." While already allowed to mandate how America's children spend the majority of their days, this practice only serves to impose further imposition and invasion into American homes on evenings and weekends. Certainly, parents want their children to be able to learn to do research, to practice new skills, to study new concepts, and to learn to prepare multi-step reports. However, after a full day of work, even most adults take a break from their jobs at the end of the day. Granted, school days are somewhat shorter in length, but consider the likely outrage that would ensue at the suggestion that students should remain in their classrooms until 5 p.m. Most Americans would consider this excessive, yet, by requiring students to fill much of their non-school time with schoolwork, it's almost the same thing.

Sure, left unsupervised with nothing to do, kids can get into trouble. But, this is not the issue. Rare is the student who buckles down to homework in the absence of adults. Instead, their homework time represents a huge interference with valuable parenting time, very necessary to maintain and strengthen child/parent bonds Too often kids are actually forced to choose between time with a parent and time cracking the books--clearly no way to encourage a love of academics. Plus, kids *need* free time. They need time to explore, to recreate, to interact with their world *without* the pressure of grades. This is a developmental *necessity* that, when inhibited, serves to stifle many students' abilities to reach their full emotional maturity.

Why is homework necessary, anyhow? It exists because there is supposedly more learning required than can reasonably be accomplished during the school day. But, what if school operated year-round instead of only nine months of the year? Considering that most American parents work, there seems to be few good reasons for schools to be closed for the entire summer, along with two full weeks in the winter, another week in the spring, and multiple days during the year. Instead of teachers being forced to try to cram all of their required instruction into only two semesters, they would have much more time for extended lessons, projects, and research, with, say, only four weeks of paid vacation, instead of the full twelve weeks most teachers currently enjoy.

If America's schools were open year round, more time during the school year could be devoted to students doing their schoolwork *in school*, under the guided supervision of trained professionals, instead of from mom and dad having to try to re-teach the lessons to their children, possibly incorrectly. Further, if there was no (or less) homework, families would be more free to plan evening and weekend activities and family outings, while also having greater freedom to assign their children greater household tasks and responsibilities. More working parents could have opportunities to volunteer at their children's schools by not having to schedule all of their vacation days when their children's schools are closed. Less starting and stopping the school year would mean more continuity of instruction. Parents would have the freedom to schedule vacations that best suited their families' needs, while schools would have to allow students more flexibility of attendance, as long as they attended for at least 11 months. As it stands now, families are completely beholden to between one and eight different teachers per child, each making demands on theirs' and their children's free time, largely so that the teachers' work year can be compressed into only 40 weeks, while they enjoy their summers off. This is a gross interference with America's civil rights that has gone on long enough and for which its reform is long overdue.

READ MORE FROM WASHINGTON D.C.:

Study: More homework not always better.

"Teachers in many nations with very high-scoring students -- Japan, the Czech Republic, Denmark -- don't assign much homework. But countries where students score poorly -- Thailand, Greece and Iran -- have teachers who assign a great deal of homework."

http://www.potomacnews.com/servlet/Satellite?pagename=WPN/MGArticle/WPN_BasicArticle&c=MGArticle&cid=1031785321320&path

---

SOLUTION 80:

ALIGN SCHOOL CALENDARS TO THE DUAL-WORK SCHEDULES OF MOST PARENTS IN THE 21ST CENTURY, NOT TO THE AGRARIAN (FARMING) SCHEDULES OF 1945.

81.

INSTRUCTION WITH NO LONG-RANGE OBJECTIVES

Each state in America has its own set of required learning (or teaching) goals, representing particular sets of knowledge that must be imparted to students in each prescribed subject area, at each grade level. Unfortunately, there is no explanation of the long-range expectations or expected outcomes for this learning. Teachers are simply supposed to provide students a particular set of information and skills, without any understanding of the particular purpose or application for the particular knowledge. This differs from most colleges, where the instructors will frequently relate their particular instruction to certain careers, while the coursework is already tied to or a particular degree. This is one more reason why so many of America's elementary and high school students, particularly from depressed regions, are so bored with school. They cannot see, and are often not provided, a purpose to learning material that often appears to have no relevance to their lives. Unless their teachers take the time to relate their instruction to long-range objectives, it seems largely meaningless to them. Unfortunately, even many teachers do not know, or have never stopped to consider, the long-range life purpose of much of their instruction for their students' futures.

READ MORE FROM BOSTON COLLEGE:

THE (UNREALIZED) PROMISE OF SCHOOL-TO-WORK EDUCATION

http://www.bc.edu/schools/law/lawreviews/meta-elements/journals/bctwj/24_2/03_FMS.htm

---

SOLUTION 81:

INSTITUTUTE ARTICULATION OF EACH SUBJECT AREA BY TEACHERS, BOTH BETWEEN GRADE AND PERFORMANCE LEVELS, WITH POST-SECONDARY COLLEGE AND CAREER REPRESENTATIVES WHO CAN CLARIFY THE USE AND APPLICATION OF THEIR INSTRUCTION IN VARIOUS CAREERS.

82.

LESSONS NOT BASED ON STUDENT NEEDS

Elaborating on the previous item, not only do teachers frequently not explain the long-range necessity of their instruction to students, the fact is, in many cases, *there is none.* This comes down to basic educational philosophy; in other words, *why* schools exist in the first place. Now, for the intellectually superior and independently wealthy, education is merely an aesthetic, an enhancement to one's already charmed life. Education in such disciplines as medieval history and French literature is merely a furthering of one's cultural superiority. However knowledge for knowledge's sake is a luxury the rest of America's students can ill-afford. Without sufficient practical and usable knowledge, most students cannot hope to rise above an entry-level job. Nevertheless, students continue to be required to know more about Attila the Hun than health insurance; more about the French Foreign Legion than financial aid; more about the Renaissance than about managing relationships. America is one of the only advanced nations that continues to require a "liberal arts" education for all students well into their late teens, rather than allowing them to pursue specific vocational or educational tracks more applicable to their post-secondary goals. Surely, were America's high schools to adopt this option, fewer kids would drop out, while more would strive to acquire the knowledge and skills that have real meaning to their own lives.

READ MORE FROM THE SHANGHAI AMERICAN SCHOOLS:

Milken Conference: "Changing post-secondary education to meet the needs of a global economy"

http://www.saschina.org

SOLUTION 82:

ALLOW HIGH SCHOOL STUDENTS THE FREEDOM TO PURSUE EDUCATION THAT IS COMPATIBLE WITH THEIR ABILITIES AND NEEDS INSTEAD OF FORCING ALL KIDS TO MAKE A 4-YEAR COLLEGE THEIR FIRST OR ONLY CONSIDERATION.

83.

ADULT LIVING SKILLS NOT TAUGHT

There are a number of informational topics for which America's youth really need more education in order to prepare them for successful adulthood; information they should really be learning in schools, particularly with the absence, today, of many full-time parents. One knowledge gap, in particular, that entraps so many students shortly after leaving school is the issue of credit. Gone are the days when one must have a well-paying full-time job in order to be issued a credit card. Predatory lenders are all to willing to extend credit to these inexperienced and immature teens, which can result in their falling into a serious financial trap before they ever even realize it.

Another subject that seems to require more learning today concerns how to manage relationships. Most high school students in America do not have the most excellent role models. They have grown up witnessing more arguments than agreements, more breakups than reconciliations, leading many to believe that anything and everything is sufficient grounds to end a relationship. Many tend to expect that their partners must always agree with them, having never learned the value of mutual respect for each other's differences.

Also, too many young adults have never learned the importance of ethics, with far too many having come to believe that any crime is acceptable as long as they can get away with it. The concept of morality and doing the right thing is almost never given sufficient attention in America's schools, largely because it is considered too difficult to teach without employing particular religious tenets, which most public schools have ruled completely prohibitive.

Finally, most students leave school with very poor verbal and written communication skills, regardless of their grades or intellect. Without some instruction in the acceptable conventions of manners, grace, and tact, America's schools are producing generations of louts, clods, and social boors who are incapable of advancing either socially or in their careers.

READ MORE FROM EDISON, NEW JERSEY:

Life Skills: What Your Schools Forgot To Teach You

http://www.primezone.com/newsroom/news.html?d=84792

SOLUTION 83:

RECOGNIZE THAT MANY STUDENTS MOVE DIRECTLY FROM HIGH SCHOOL TO ADULTHOOD AND ENSURE THAT THEY ARE ADEQUATELY INFORMED IN ALL ASPECTS OF CONSUMER PITFALLS AND ETHICAL EXPECTATIONS.

84.

SPECIAL EDUCATION: "WHAT'S SO SPECIAL?"

While an elaborate system of rules and laws were developed in the 1970's, and then expanded in the 1990's, to improve education to students with disabilities, in reality there is actually nothing special about *"special education."* With the exception of a few highly-specialized services provided in very rare instances to very few students, special education is nothing more than an excuse for substandard teaching by under-qualified teachers in a segregated manner to students who need more, not less, expertise. Sure, there are certification standards for teachers of numerous disability categories. However, these teachers are not dually trained in the subject areas that they teach. For example, a teacher of high school chemistry, instructing students with learning disabilities in a separate special education classroom, is only required to be trained in "learning disabilities," not in chemistry. This is equally true with all other subject areas currently being taught by special education teachers of any and all school subjects.

Special education typically is not a temporary "fix," like braces, to bring students up to the achievement level of their same-aged peers. Once children are "identified" as disabled by their schools, it is a slippery slope. Because the pace of the instruction is then slowed, most will *never* be able to catch up. They might have half a chance if they were allowed to attend school over the summers to catch up, but, unless they are found to be at serious risk of "regression," (e.g. forgetting most of what they already learned); they are not usually entitled to summer services. Further, as this example illustrates, a number of decisions are allowed to be made by schools related to their special education students that are in the best interests of the *schools*, and not these kids. There is currently legislation before the federal courts citing the contradictory premise of the No Child Left Behind law and the Individuals with Disabilities Education Act, due to the former requiring that *all students must perform at grade level*, while the latter is based on the fact that many do not.

In reality, it is the special education students in the majority of America's schools who are provided the scarcest resources, the least new textbooks, and the fewest opportunities to participate in school activities. Originally invented as a response to schools' expanded legal obligation to educate *all children*, the needs of America's disabled students have continually taken a backseat to schools' primary mission, while these students are regarded predominantly as a burden on schools' resources.

READ MORE FROM THE NEW YORK DAILY NEWS:
Special ed kids shortchanged.

"Nearly nine out of every 10 special education students in city schools fail to earn a high school diploma."

http://www.nydailynews.com/news/local/v-pfriendly/story/315490p-269876c.html

SOLUTION 84:

PERMIT THE MORE CAPABLE STUDENTS TO MOVE AHEAD VIA SELF-DIRECTED LEARNING AND REDUCE P.E. AND OTHER NON-ACADEMIC SUBJECTS TO EXTRA-CURRICULAR STATUS, FREEING UP MORE TEACHERS TO PROVIDE GREATER INDIVIDUALIZED INSTRUCTION TO THE STUDENTS WHO NEED IT MOST.

85.

"DISABILITY" MEANS "DISCARDED EXPECTATIONS"

At the same time "special education" is viewed as an unnecessary burden by many educators, it is, nevertheless, utilized quite frequently as a "dumping ground" for the students that America's schools have failed to educate sufficiently, properly, or in a timely manner. An overwhelming number of students who cannot read by the third grade are identified as "learning disabled" by the fourth grade, based on some loosely defined criteria that are far from scientific. Students exhibiting any amount of "unacceptable" behaviors are at risk of being labeled as "behavior disordered," which can result in their being removed to a separate classroom or school, to teachers trained in managing behaviors, but not in any of the academic subjects they teach.

READ MORE FROM THE ARIZONA DAILY STAR:

Special Education: For disabled (and abled).
"The federal government guarantees all special-needs students a free public education in the least restrictive and most appropriate setting. But federal funding has never covered more than a fraction of the cost."

http://www.azstarnet.com/clips/specialed.htm

SOLUTION 85:

ALLOW NO SPECIAL ED ELIGIBILITY TO BE DETERMINED BY SCHOOL PSYCHOLOGISTS BEHOLDEN TO THEIR SCHOOS, BUT ONLY BY LICENSED PHYSICIANS, SIGNIFANTLY LIMITING ARBITRARY AND CAPRICIOUS "DISABILITY" DETERMINATIONS THAT EXCUSE SCHOOLS FROM RESPONSIBILITY FOR INADEQUATE TEACHING.

86.

DISABLED STUDENTS: MISIDENTIFIED, OVER-IDENTIFICATIFIED, UNDER-EDUCATED

While the more obvious categories of disability, including Hearing Impaired, Visually Impaired, Physically Handicapped, and Mentally Impaired students typically receive an education that is at least somewhat compatible with their learning needs, the overwhelming majority of students designated for "special education" are labeled as "learning disabled" or "emotionally/behaviorally disordered," categories that are so vague as to be ripe for misuse. Students who are less "teachable" than their classmates are all too eagerly identified as "disabled" by their schools due to federal and state laws permitting entirely too much leeway in diagnostic criteria.

Once placed into "special" education, be it a separate classroom or added supports in a regular class setting, rarely are these students actually provided any instructional supports that are "specialized" in any manner. With very few exceptions, special education services are anything but special. They represent a very limited list of identical supports being provided to all "special" students, while utilizing lower-level curricula, regardless of the students' individual disability or need. It's a slower track; period. In reality, this is the full extent of specialized instruction most of America's schools are able to accomplish. Schools were designed to service *groups*, not individuals. If most schools in America promise parents anything more in terms of resources, services, or man hours, chances are it's not happening, at least not as consistently as promised. One reason is that special education administrators are not usually housed in the same building as the teachers delivering the services, and the principals are generally completely unaware of what the teachers are supposed to be doing for these students.

READ MORE FROM VIRGINIA DEPARTMENT OF EDUCATION:

Disproportional Identification of EBD

The Problem of Disproportionate Representation in Special Education for Students with EBD

http://johnl.edschool.virginia.edu/blogs/ebdblog/2005/05/03/disproportionality/

SOLUTION 86:

ELIMINATE "GRADE-LEVELS" AND GROUP STUDENTS BY ABILITY LEVELS, WITH GREATER EMPHASIS ON STUDENT PROGRESS THAN ON ARTIFICIALLY-STATED ACHIEVEMENT IN "9TH GRADE MATH" THAT USES "4TH GRADE" TEXTBOOKS.

87.

INCLUSION: NO ONE PREPARED THE "INCLUDING" TEACHERS

One more word on special education -- and that word is "inclusion." It's the new buzz word in education. It means "including" students with disabilities in the same classes as their non-disabled peers. The idea is that rather than providing disabled students specialized education geared to their specific intellectual and academic needs, students should, instead, be included in "regular" classes with "appropriate academic supports." The problem with this ideal is that *no one asked the regular education teachers.*

Unfortunately, not only were they not trained in how to adapt their instruction to meet the needs of these students, many are now expected to "co-teach" with a special education teacher. However, no one defined exactly how these "co-taught" classes are supposed to work. If only the regular education teacher is knowledgeable in the subject area, does that relegate the special education teacher to the role of "assistant?" Further, if students with disabilities are not to be singled out and specifically identified, how is the special education teacher supposed to teach only to them in the regular education class? These are just two examples of numerous problems with this practice. Many teachers have chosen, instead, to simply resist the entire concept. Those who have been teaching long enough have been subjected to numerous educational "experiments" that are deemed mandatory one year, and then cast by the wayside the next year. Seasoned teachers, therefore, have grown to believe that no school change lasts, and if they simply resist long enough they can retire before ever being forced to adopt the latest new mandate.

READ MORE FROM CITY UNIVERSITY OF NEW YORK:

Full Inclusion: A False Remedy to a National Dilemma

http://maxweber.hunter.cuny.edu/cgi-bin/eres/bboardread.pl?EDSPC753_MCINTYRE!13!4

SOLUTION 87:

ELIMINATE SEPARATE CERTIFICATION OF "SPECIAL" EDUCATION TEACHERS, AND, INSTEAD, REQUIRE ALL TEACHERS TO COMPLETE TRAINING IN THE DELIVERY OF SPECIFIC SUBJECT AREAS TO STUDENTS WITH DISABILITIES, THEREBY ELIMINATING THE NEED FOR SPECIAL EDUCATION TEACHERS WHO LACK SUBJECT-MATTER TRAINING, AS WELL AS REGULAR EDUCATION TEACHERS WHO "CAN'T" TEACH STUDENTS WITH DISABILITIES.

THE STUDENTS:

"WHO'S REALLY RESPONSIBLE?"

88.

NO ONE GRADES THE TEACHERS

If a 4th grade math teacher decides to skip over teaching long-division due to insufficient knowledge, skill or time, no one will really care. That is, no one will care enough to take any specific action against the teacher. Mostly because, chances are, no one will ever *know*. Instead, whenever a child fails to demonstrate a particular academic skill, America's schools use every other possible excuse before ever attributing this failure to the teacher; from poor parenting to poor social environment to poor attendance to poor prenatal care. Chances are that the school principal will never know since most only observe teachers once or twice per year. The superintendent and school board members will never know because students' standardized test scores, on which schools' performance is measured, are (intentionally?) not tied to specific teachers. Finally, most parents will never know, but will, instead, be surprised when their child fails to achieve college admission status in math on their SATs years later. Education is the only industry where there is absolutely no correlation made between employee effort and outcomes.

READ MORE FROM THE PITTSBURGH POST-GAZETTE:
<u>Teacher tests zapped again; Classroom performance not measured, researcher says</u>
http://www.post-gazette.com/regionstate/20020123teachertest0123p5.asp

---

<u>*SOLUTION 88*</u>:

EVALUATE TEACHER COMPETENCY ON THEIR STUDENTS' ACHIEVEMENT IN EACH PRESCRIBED BENCHMARK FOR THEIR SUBJECT AREA(S.

89.

"THE TEACHERS ARE NOT RESPONSIBLE"

The thing is, even if teachers are *known* to have skipped key concepts in their instruction, they still would have little to fear, since, despite the mandate of federal and state learning goals, that's all they are; "goals." While the identified instructional concepts must be included in a school's curricula, and, therefore, in teachers' written "lesson plans," teachers are not evaluated for instructional consistency or compatibility with learning goals throughout the school year, only for their ability to deliver one or two carefully planned lessons. Ironically, these observations are actually called *"Performance* Evaluations," and performances they usually are. It would typically take years for school administrators to detect that a particular teacher is actually incompetent to teach a subject using this limited means of assessment, but by then the teacher would have likely earned tenure, thereby insulating them from termination for anything short of a felony. Still, as an even further protection from reprisal, most teachers can easily manipulate students' grades to mask their own teaching deficiencies. Finally, there are typically always a few "self-teachers" in any class, students who manage to either teach themselves the missed instruction, or who entered the class already in possession of the required knowledge, serving to further shield a teacher's lack of ability in either case.

READ MORE FROM THE NEW YORK TIMES:

No high school student left behind

"The American high school is a big part of the problem. Developed a century ago, the standard factory-style high school was conceived as a combination holding area and sorting device that would send roughly one-fifth of its students on to college while moving the rest directly into low-skill jobs."

http://www.erinoconnor.org/archives/2005/02/no_high_school.html

---

SOLUTION 89:

TRAIN SCHOOL ADMINISTRATORS IN MEANS OF ACCURATELY ASSESSING A TEACHER'S ABILITY TO TEACH, NOT MERELY PERFORM.

90.

PARENTS GET NOT GOVERNMENTAL PROTECTION

By now, many readers may be thinking, "Why worry?" After all, America's schools are subject to state and federal regulation and governance. It's generally assumed that there are laws in place to protect students from educational malpractice, and that the state education agencies exist to protect students, under the watchful eye of the U.S. Department of Education. Wrong! Not only are there far too many schools, committing far too many offenses, for any state agency to ever manage them all, the truth is, most state departments of education don't even see this as their *role*. Instead, they gladly pass the buck to the local school boards made up mostly of non-educators, unfamiliar with many school laws. States education agencies, meanwhile, perform only perfunctory and superficial monitoring of schools, typically only once every four years or so, when they often do little more than require school districts to submit their own self-selected examples of student records. Federal oversight of states' educational practices is even less impressive.

Although the originators of most legislation related to Special Education and "No child left behind," federal monitoring of each state's educational practices is limited to once every seven years, while often only visiting one or two schools in an entire state before declaring it compliant.

READ MORE FROM THE OHIO DEPARTMENT OF EDUCATION:

Whose IDEA Is This?

http://olrs.ohio.gov/asp/WhoseIDEAFAQ2.asp

SOLUTION 90:

ALLOW FEWER DEVIATIONS FROM NATIONAL STANDARDS SO THAT MEASURES OF SCHOOL ACHIEVEMENT ARE SUFFICIENTLY REGULATED TO REVEAL ANY SIGNIFICANT DEPARTURES FROM ACCEPTABLE SCHOOL PERFORMANCE.

91.

PARENTS' RIGHTS: KEPT HIDDEN FROM VIEW

Parents do have rights with regard to their children's education in America's schools, but schools, for the most part, go out of their way to keep these rights obscured from view. For example, most school administrators do not want it made known that parents have a right to visit their children's classrooms, to question a teacher's instructional methods and grading, to demand instruction compatible with their child's learning needs, or to protest school policies that seem unjust or harmful.

Many parents fail to understand the role of their local school boards in exerting their rights. What many need to realize is that these are the only *elected* officials in their schools' hierarchy, who are beholden, first and foremost, to their constituents to uphold appropriate educational practices. Rather than being available to parents, however, many school boards tend to be somewhat elitist and inaccessible groups. Nevertheless, parents should know that when seeking a school's cooperation, communicating with one's State education agency is not nearly as expedient or effective as bringing one's dissatisfaction to the attention of their local school board members. The last thing these individuals want is dissatisfied potential voters, and will, therefore, exert pressure on schools to compel their immediate cooperation.

READ MORE FROM THE NEW YORK TIMES:

School Cellphone Ban Violates Rights of Parents, Lawsuit Says

http://www.nytimes.com/2006/07/14/nyregion/14phones.html?ei=5090&en=2b8460f55e5cbc67&ex=1310529600&partner=rssuserland&emc=rss&pagewanted=print

---

SOLUTION 91:

MAINTAIN A PARENT EDUCATION FORUM IN EACH STATE WHERE ISSUES ARE OPENLY DISCUSSED, EXPERIENCES ARE SHARED, RIGHTS ARE CLARIFIED, AND LEGAL GUIDANCE IS PROVIDED.

92.

REGIONAL OFFICES OF EDUCATION "ARTIFICIAL" AUTHORITIES

In many states, in addition to State Offices of Education, there are *Regional Offices of Education* (ROEs) as well, purportedly in place to provide more accessibility and immediate State support to students and their parents. This is, in fact, rarely the case. While these state-supported offices typically provide a handful of services to educators, they are largely a useless waste of taxpayers' money for their facilities, staff, and services that do little to enhance the education of students, while the majority of their services to educators could be more easily provided via the internet.

READ MORE FROM THE HERITAGE FOUNDATION:

Why Congress Should Overhaul the Federal Regional Education Laboratories

http://www.heritage.org/research/education/BG1200.cfm

SOLUTION 92:

ELIMINATE REGIONAL OFFICES OF EDUCATION, SAVING STATES MILLIONS OF DOLLARS, AND REDIRECT THESE RESOURCES TO THE LOCAL SCHOOLS.

93.

SCHOOL MALPRACTICE & OTHER CRIMES AGAINST STUDENTS

Unlike the practice of medicine, which affects the human body, the practice of education, which affects the preservation of the human mind, carries no criminal penalties whatsoever for malpractice. There is no *"Hippocratic Oath"* for teachers, no moral credo compelling them to always teach in an appropriate and sufficient manner. Sadly, there are actually more opportunities today to correct most medical mistakes than to reverse the cognitive impairments resulting from substandard or inaccurate instruction, often not detected until years later, after the students' developmental milestones have already passed.

Speaking of criminality, while more and more educators are being found guilty of multiple offenses involving their students, including sexual improprieties, there remain in countless schools throughout America literally thousands of teachers, administrators, janitors, and others, gainfully employed by schools, who have already been discovered to have committed some type of illegal or inappropriate act with or in their presence of children, but who were simply offered the opportunity to resign by their former schools in lieu of any further investigation. Because of the amount of time, trouble, and bad publicity involved in proving most of these cases, many school leaders elect to simply remove, reassign, or encourage the resignation of, the offending educators, resulting in their being free to continue their criminal patterns in other schools.

Finally, it may surprise most to know that there is typically no drug testing of school personnel. Further, there are a number of felony convictions that do not preclude someone from being employed as a teacher in America.

READ MORE FROM THE WASHINGTON POST:

A Chart Exposes High School Malpractice

"Students who struggle in an AP course . . . are still much better off than if they had been denied a chance to take the course and the test."

http://www.washingtonpost.com/wpdyn/articles/A6900-2004Nov23.html

---

SOLUTION 93:

HOLD EDUCATORS RESPONSIBLE FOR MISSED INSTRUCTION AFFECTING STUDENT PROGRESS. HOLD SCHOOLS, LIKE CHURCHES AND OTHER INSTITUTIONS, RESPONSIBLE FOR CONCEALING THE CRIMINAL ACTIVITIES COMMITTED AGAINST CHILDREN BY THEIR EMPLOYEES. HOLD THOSE EMPLOYED BY SCHOOLS TO THE HIGHEST STANDARD OF PROFESSIONAL "CLEARANCE."

THE OUTCOMES:

"WHAT GOOD IS IT?"

94.

ARBITRARY PROMOTIONS

When a student is promoted from one grade to the next, one can only assume that they have demonstrated sufficient achievement in all required academic areas of the previous grade. This is often not so. America's schools merely require that students demonstrate "passing grades" in the *majority* of their subjects, for the *majority* of the school year to be considered to have "passed" a particular grade. "Passing" to the next grade does not typically require that the student earned a passing grade in all of the required subject areas. Further, the criteria for earning a "passing grade" in a given subject is almost always at the sole discretion of the *teacher*, instead of being based on any objective standards, with teachers frequently including a number of subjective criteria in calculating their students' final "letter grades." These factors actually serve to render letter grades meaningless, yet America's schools place the greatest importance on these arbitrary performance indicators, well above students' actual performance on any standardized measure of academic achievement. In high school, these arbitrary letter grades serve as the basis for students' grade point averages and class ranks, which carry even greater weight than SATs in determining most students' admission into most colleges.

READ MORE FROM RANCHO PENASQUITOS, CA:

Westview High boosts GPAs for AP test-takers

"Some parents and teachers contend that [the school] is inflating grades and creating an unfair advantage for their college-bound students over other students."

http://www.signonsandiego.com/news/education/200503 16-9999-1mi16grades.html

---

SOLUTION 94:

STOP THE ARBITRARY ASSIGNMENT OF LETTER GRADES BASED ON SUBJECTIVE CRITERIA AND LIMIT ALL OUTWARD EXPRESSIONS OF STUDENTS' ACADEMIC PERFORMANCE TO THAT WHICH CAN BE DEEMED VALID AND RELIABLE.

95.

GRADES BASED ON BEHAVIOR, NOT LEARNING

Continuing with the subject of grading, not only is the criterion subjective, it is almost always based more on students' behavior than on their mastery of the particular subject matter. This includes how well a student followed directions, the length of their essays, the number of math problems they completed for homework, and the number of times they were tardy to class. At the risk of being repetitious, let me say again: *There are no State learning goals for behavior!* While teachers may need to learn other means of managing students' behavior, their students' academic grades, are meant only to represent each student's level of *academic* achievement, and so are intended to be representative of how much a student learned about a subject area within a certain period of time. Nothing more, or less.

READ MORE FROM Pennsylvania, Kentucky, New York, California, Missouri, Texas:

Grades: What Do They Mean?

http://www.middleweb.com/MWLISTCONT/MSLgrading.html

SOLUTION 95:

DISCONTINUE THE CONSIDERATION OF SUBJECTIVE CRITERIA IN CALCULATING OR REPORTING STUDENTS' ACADEMIC ACHIEVEMENT AND LIMIT THE ASSIGNMENT OF "LETTER GRADES" TO EQUITABLE STANDARDS, ONLY.

96.

A "D" IS GOOD ENOUGH

Somewhere past kindergarten, but before high school, most students' grades begin being expressed in the traditional "A through F" format. We all know what each letter represents; a level of demonstrated knowledge in a particular subject area, from "Superior," to "Above Average," to "Average," to "Below Average," to "Failure." These letter grades are also correlated to particular percentages of achievement. Typically, 90% or better is required for an A, 80% or better for a B, 70% or better for a C, 60% or better for a D, and 59% or less for an F. Unfortunately, this very familiar system of grading allows for a rather disturbing premise . . . that a student could continually learn only 60% of the prescribed material in any required subject and still be considered to have learned enough to "*pass*," that is, to be able to advance to the next level of instruction. This practice, however, can only result in a snowball effect of eventual failure as students are moved ahead who have failed to achieve sufficient mastery in multiple areas. In order to ensure an appropriate level of learning, while also holding America's teachers and schools more accountable for their instruction, no student should be considered to have *passed* any subject until the have demonstrated learning of *at least* 80% of the material. For parents, educators, or taxpayers to accept anything less is to permit students to advance who have not shown that the instruction benefited them at all.

READ MORE FROM JACKSONVILLE, FL:

Thousands of students victims of 'grade inflation'

http://schoolmatch.com/audit/jacksonville/articles/grade zz.htm

---

SOLUTION 96:

BASING STUDENTS' PROGRESSION TO THE NEXT LEVEL OF INSTRUCTION STRICTLY ON STANDARDIZED MEASUREMENTS OF ACHIEVEMENT, WHILE ESTABLISHING MINIMUM STANDARDS OF ACADEMIC GAIN, WOULD ELIMINATE THE CHARADE OF "PASSING GRADES."

97.

UNEQUAL GRADUATION REQUIREMENTS

What is An American high school diploma? Does it have any consistent value from one school to the next? Many Americans might find it surprising to learn that the classes required for graduation can vary from school to school, and from town to town, even within the same county. Yet, having a "high school diploma" means the difference between virtually all career and college entrance. It is one of the primary benchmarks of achievement upon which America's very society is based. Shouldn't there, then, at least be some consistency in what is required to earn this very important credential? Instead, to make matters worse, in some schools where a state's or district's graduation requirements are perceived as too rigid, there is an unspoken policy of "substituting" easier courses for the more difficult required ones, while the required course titles remain on the students' transcript, often without the knowledge of the parents' or the receiving colleges. In any other industry this would be recognized for what it is: fraud.

READ MORE FROM NORTH DAKOTA:

Restore Value to the High School Diploma

"In every state today, students can meet the requirements for high school graduation and still be unprepared for success in college or the workplace."

http://www.ndus.nodak.edu/uploads/document-library/773/8D--RESTORE-VALUE-TO-THE-HIGH-SCHOOL-DIPLOMA--ACHIEVE.PDF#search='different%20high%20school%20graduation%20requirements%20from%20school%20to%20school'

SOLUTION 97:

ESTABLISH NATIONAL HIGH SCHOOL GRADUATION REQUIREMENTS, WITH TWO COMPLETION OPTIONS, A "COLLEGE-BOUND" TRACK AND A "VOCATIONAL" TRACK. STUDENTS COMPLETING THE VOCATIONAL TRACK COULD STILL GO TO COLLEGE, BUT MIGHT NEED TO ATTEND JUNIOR COLLEGE FIRST, IN ORDER TO MAKE UP ANY COURSE DEFICIENCIES.

98.

STUDENT FAILURES ARE NEVER THE TEACHER'S FAULT

When a salesman fails to sell, he doesn't blame the customer, when a fisherman fails to catch a fish, he doesn't blame the fish, but when a teacher fails to teach it's the *students* who get the blame, along with their parents. Teachers are almost never considered to be the reason for a student's failing to learn. Rather than recognizing that students are naturally drawn to learn anything that is made interesting and relatable, America's students' failure to learn is continually blamed on everything from bad parenting to income level, to race, to gender, to food allergies, to a "learning disability," a concept largely invented to explain and justify poor teaching. *What about America's schools recognizing a "teaching disability" as another very possible explanation of students' failures?"* Nevertheless, regardless of whether anyone learns, teachers are still accorded generous automatic annual raises.

READ MORE FROM CALIFORNIA:

Teachers who don't teach – the next radical "education" idea.

http://www.kimberlyswygert.com/archives/002585.html

SOLUTION 98:

INCORPORATE PROVEN BEST EDUCATIONAL PRACTICES FOR ALL SUBJECT AREAS AND REQUIRE MORE OF THESE METHODS INTO TEACHER TRAINING.

99.

"REINVENTING THE WHEEL" WASTES TIME AND TALENT

America's schools' practice of "re-inventing the wheel" in each school, rather than sharing and using systems, curricula, and teaching methods that have already been proven to work best, is a common theme repeated frequently throughout America's educational systems. This results in countless unnecessary expenditures being authorized to re-create lessons and re-assess programs that have already been created and assessed. It's time for America's schools to get out of their 20th century rut and face the educational challenges of the 21st century. America's students, living in the richest, most powerful, most technologically and scientifically advanced nation in the world, deserve nothing less.

READ MORE FROM SOUTHWESTERN NEW MEXICO ALLIANCE FOR LEARNING:

The Principles that effective schools have in common:

http://www.wnmu.org/academic/mat/tesol/consult/Articles/ReLearning.html

SOLUTION 99:

SPEND NOT ONE MORE AMERICAN EDUCATION DOLLAR ON ANY RESOURCES OR INFORMATION ALREADY READILY AVAILABLE TO SCHOOLS FOR FREE.

100.

AMERICA'S SCHOOLS: "WHAT"S REALLY THE POINT?"

Across the land there is a huge disparity between America's schools, with those needing resources the most continuing to have the least, while the schools producing the highest student test scores continuing to enjoy the most and best resources to educate their students who would likely produce these scores whether they attended school or not. Nevertheless, America compels its parents to send their children to school for a minimum of 10 to 12 years; in short, for their entire childhoods. It's a governmental indoctrination, a national enculturation, a "communistic-like" directive, in a nation otherwise grounded in democracy. Resistance is both difficult and costly, and requires much parental sacrifice, while resisting sending one's children to school is not necessarily in their best interests, either. School in America represents the largest component of children's socialization with their peers, while, when done correctly, also affords them much needed instruction in all core subject areas. It's not that most parents want America's schools to be eliminated, only that they become less rigid and more amenable to the needs of individual students and families. They believe that schools should be more fair, equitable, and accountable for student learning. In short, most feel that America's schools should exist to serve students, not the other way around.

READ MORE FROM "PUBLIC EDUCATION, THE POINT OF NO RETURN: ARE WE THERE?"

from Samuel L. Blumenfeld book, <u>NEA: Trojan Horse in American Education</u>.

http://www.sntp.net/education/no_return.htm

SOLUTION 100:

ENSURE THAT, WITHOUT EXCEPTION, ALL STUDENTS IN AMERICA RECEIVE ALL OF THE BENEFITS FROM THEIR SCHOOLS ACCORDED TO ANY OTHER STUDENTS DURING THE SCHOOL DAY, INCLUDING ADEQUATE AND APPROPRIATE INSTRUCTION IN ALL REQUIRED SUBJECT AREAS. IF SCHOOLS WITH MORE RESOURCES SEEK TO PROVIDE SUPPLEMENTAL EDUCATIONAL OPPORTUNITIES NOT AVAILABLE IN ALL SCHOOLS, THESE MUST BE PROVIDED THROUGH ALTERNATIVE PROGRAMMING AND NOT BE INCLUDED IN THE REGULAR SCHOOL DAY OR BUDGET. THAT WAY, NO STUDENT IN ANY SCHOOL IN AMERICA WILL BE DENIED THEIR RIGHTS TO AN EQUAL AND HIGH-QUALITY EDUCATION.

Student's Bill of Rights

I have the right to learn at my own pace and not feel put down or stupid if I'm slower than anyone else.

I have the right to be treated as a competent individual.

I have the right to view myself as a competent individual.

I have the right to dislike any particular subject, even though my goals require its mastery.

I have the right to feel good about myself, regardless of my abilities in any particular subject.

I have the right to evaluate my teachers and how they teach.

I have the right not to understand.

I have the right to say I don't understand.

I have the right to ask whatever questions I have.

I have the right to need extra help.

I have the right to ask a teacher or teacher's aide for help.

I have the right to define success as determined by my effort.

I have the right not to base my self-worth on my skill in any particular area.

I have the right to relax.

(From: http://www.visionhelp.com/rights.htm)

Have a question, problem, or dilemma with one of America's schools?

Need an answer to a school problem or want to share your school experiences with others?

Feel free to submit your questions and

"School horror stories" to

kploftus@outcomes4learning.com

Read more commentaries on America's Schools by Dr. Loftus and others at
www.EducationNews.org

Watch for

<u>Stolen Chances: 100 More Things Wrong with America's Schools</u>

due out in early 2007

About the Author

Dr. Loftus is a mother of four, a school administrator, and the director of Outcomes Educational Services, a parent advocacy, educator training, and student support organization in the Chicago suburbs. She is also a regular columnist on topics of school reform with EducationNews. (www.educationnews.org.)

Being both an experienced educator and State of Illinois monitor of schools' special education compliance, Dr. Loftus is also recognized as an outspoken whistleblower of violations to students' educational rights. While actively working to improve education for all children, she continues to conduct research and provide commentary on contemporary issues in American education that are serving as barriers to both student learning and growth.

www.ingramcontent.com/pod-product-compliance
Lightning Source LLC
Chambersburg PA
CBHW020751160426
43192CB00006B/296